Using Children's Literature in Preschool to Develop Comprehension

Understanding and Enjoying Books

2ND EDITION

LESLEY MANDEL MORROW
ELIZABETH FREITAG
LINDA B. GAMBRELL

Part of the Preschool Literacy Collection edited by
Lesley Mandel Morrow

INTERNATIONAL
Reading Association
800 BARKSDALE ROAD, PO BOX 8139
NEWARK, DE 19714-8139, USA
www.reading.org

The International Reading Association attempts, through its publications, to provide a forum for a wide spectrum of opinions on reading. This policy permits divergent viewpoints without implying the endorsement of the Association.

Executive Editor, Books   Corinne M. Mooney
Developmental Editor   Charlene M. Nichols
Developmental Editor   Tori Mello Bachman
Developmental Editor   Stacey L. Reid
Editorial Production Manager   Shannon T. Fortner
Design and Composition Manager   Anette Schuetz
Project Editor   Stacey L. Reid

Cover   Design, Monotype; Photograph, Douglas H. Bushell

Library of Congress Cataloging-in-Publication Data
Morrow, Lesley Mandel.
    Using children's literature in preschool to develop comprehension: understanding and enjoying books/Lesley Mandel Morrow, Elizabeth Freitag, and Linda B. Gambrell. -- 2nd ed.
        p. cm. -- (Preschool literacy collection)
    Rev. ed. of: Using children's literature in preschool.
    Includes bibliographical references and index.
    ISBN 978-0-87207-474-3
    1. Language arts (Preschool)--United States. 2. Reading (Preschool)--United States. 3. Children--Books and reading--United States. I. Freitag, Elizabeth. II. Gambrell, Linda B. III. Morrow, Lesley Mandel. Using children's literature in preschool. IV. International Reading Association. V. Title.
    LB1140.5.L3M67 2009
    372.64--dc22   2008048307

To all the teachers who read to their children and helped them to love books.

CONTENTS

Lesley Mandel Morrow is a Professor of Literacy at Rutgers University's Graduate School of Education in New Brunswick, New Jersey, USA, where she is chair of the Department of Learning and Teaching. She began her career as a classroom teacher, then became a reading specialist, and later received her PhD from Fordham University in New York City. Her area of research focuses on strategies for enhancing early literacy development and the organization and management of language arts programs. Her research is conducted with children and families from diverse backgrounds.

Morrow has more than 300 publications that include journal articles, book chapters, monographs, and books. She received Excellence in Research, Teaching, and Service awards from Rutgers University. She was the recipient of the International Reading Association's (IRA) Outstanding Teacher Educator of Reading Award and Fordham University's Alumni Award for Outstanding Achievement. In addition, Morrow has received numerous grants for research from the U.S. federal government and has served as a principal research investigator for the Center of English Language Arts, National Reading Research Center, and the Center for Early Reading Achievement.

Presently, Morrow is a principal investigator for the Mid-Atlantic Regional Lab, funded by the U.S. Department of Education and New York University Medical School's BELLE Project: The Preparation of Disadvantaged Preschoolers for Language and Literacy Success during Pediatric Primary Care, funded by the National Institute of Child Health and Human Development. She was an elected member of the IRA Board of Directors and served as president of the organization in 2003–2004. She was elected into the Reading Hall of Fame in 2006.

Elizabeth Freitag graduated Phi Beta Kappa from Rutgers, the State University of New Jersey in New Brunswick, New Jersey, USA. After graduation, she worked in after-school programs in urban settings before returning to Rutgers to pursue a master's degree in elementary education. As a graduate student, she was awarded an

Educational Testing Service Teacher Scholarship and an Executive Women of New Jersey Graduate Merit Award. In addition to the work Freitag contributed to this edition, she designed the classroom activity pages at the conclusion of *Literacy Development in the Early Years: Helping Children Read and Write* (6th ed.) by Lesley Mandel Morrow.

 Linda B. Gambrell is Distinguished Professor of Education in the Eugene T. Moore School of Education at Clemson University in Clemson, South Carolina, USA, where she teaches graduate and undergraduate literacy courses. Prior to coming to Clemson University in 1999, she was Associate Dean for Research in the College of Education at the University of Maryland at College Park. She began her career as an elementary classroom teacher and reading specialist in Prince George's County, Maryland. From 1992–1997, she was principal investigator at the National Reading Research Center, University of Maryland, where she directed the Literacy Motivation Project. She has served as an elected member of the Board of Directors of the IRA, National Reading Conference, and College Reading Association, and has served as president of all three organizations.

Gambrell's major research areas are literacy motivation, the role of discussion in teaching and learning, and comprehension strategy instruction. She has authored or coauthored 10 books and more than 100 chapters and journal articles on literacy. Her research has been published in major scholarly journals, including *Reading Research Quarterly*, *Educational Psychologist*, and *Journal of Educational Research*. She has served on the editorial review boards of the most prestigious peer-reviewed journals in the field of literacy. She has served as coeditor of *The Journal of Reading Behavior*, a publication of the National Reading Conference, and *Literacy Teaching and Learning: An International Journal of Reading and Writing*.

Gambrell has received professional honors and awards, including the College Reading Association A.B. Herr Award for Outstanding Contributions to the Field of Reading, 1994; International Reading Association Outstanding Teacher Educator in Reading Award, 1998; National Reading Conference Albert J. Kingston Award, 2001; College Reading Association Laureate Award, 2002; Outstanding Faculty Member in Research, Eugene T. Moore School of Education, 2008; and in 2004 she was inducted into the Reading Hall of Fame.

GLOSSARY

This glossary provides definitions for many of the specialized literacy terms in this book. These terms are highlighted in boldface type on first occurrence.

assessment: Gathering relevant information to document a child's learning and growth.

comprehension: The ability to read or listen to and understand text as being one of the major goals of reading instruction.

concepts of books: Learning about the parts of a book, such as the front and back covers, title page, print, and pictures; this also involves learning about how to handle a book.

Directed Listening–Thinking Activity (DLTA)/Directed Reading–Thinking Activity (DRTA): Programs that provide activities and strategies utilized by teachers and students to retrieve information through pre-questioning, discussion, setting a purpose for reading a story, and post-reading discussion.

dramatic play: An advanced form of play in which children take on roles and act out make-believe stories and situations.

echo reading: The teacher reads a line of text, and then the children read the same line.

emergent literacy: A child's early, unconventional attempts at reading, writing, and listening, such as scribble writing and pretend reading.

English-language learner: Child whose first language is not English and who may be at a different level of proficiency in English.

language: A verbal system that consists of words and rules for organizing words and changing them.

literacy: A written system of marks that "fixes" language in place so it can be saved. It involves reading, writing, and the thinking needed to produce and comprehend texts.

phonological awareness: Understanding that oral language has structure that is separate from meaning.

picture walk: Flipping through the pages of a book with a child to introduce the story and generate interest.

repeated reading: Reading the same story often, each time to reinforce a different skill.

retelling: The process in which a reader, having orally read a story, describes what happened in it.

scaffolding: The process whereby a child's learning occurs in the context of full performance as adults gradually relinquish support.

shared reading: A classroom strategy in which a teacher reads a Big Book with enlarged print and encourages the children to read along on parts that they can remember or predict. Shared reading models the reading process and draws children's attention to print concepts and letter knowledge.

syntactic complexity: The complexity of grammatical patterns or structures.

thematic unit: Using a themed topic, such as the study of plants using science, to teach about that topic in art, music, social studies, math, reading, writing, listening, speaking, and play.

think-aloud: Asking children to visualize what they see after they have been read to. They discuss the images with peers and predict what will happen next in the story.

vocabulary: The words children know and use.

writing center: A classroom area stocked with materials that invite children to engage in writing.

ACKNOWLEDGMENTS

The authors acknowledge Kristin Valvanis for taking photographs and her help with editing. We also thank Thu Win and Anna Turkenich for their editing support.

CHAPTER 1

Why Comprehension of Children's Literature Is Important in Preschool

• • • • • • • • • • • • • •

Ms. King's preschool classroom of 3- and 4-year-olds is outside playing on the playground when it begins to snow. It is the first snow of the year, and the children are quite excited. Four-year-old Kyle says, "Look, there is a flake on my jacket!" Some children cup their hands to catch the flakes, and others open up their mouths and lean their heads back to let the flakes fall on their tongues. The snow is falling fast in big flakes, and it covers the ground in minutes. Children start to write their names and draw pictures in the snow on the ground. It seems to be getting colder and windy, so Ms. King suggests it is time to go inside.

Taking advantage of this event when they return to the classroom, Ms. King picks out the book *The Snowy Day* by Ezra Jack Keats (1998) to read to the children, saying, "Look what I found, it is a book about snow." The children come to the **literacy** center to listen to the read-aloud. Ms. King has a Big Book version on an easel so the children can easily see the words and the illustrations. Before reading, Ms. King tells the children that the story is about a little boy named Peter who goes out into the snow and does a lot of things. She asks them to try to remember one or two of the things he does. She also says that every time she says the /sss/ sound, that is their clue to say the word *snow*. Then she will write the word on the experience chart next to her.

The children listen very attentively to remember what things Peter did in the snow, and every time Ms. King looks at them and says the /sss/ sound, they chime in and say the word *snow*.

Ms. King reads, "One winter morning Peter woke up and looked out the window. Sssss…[everyone says *snow*] had fallen during the night. It covered everything as far as he could see. After breakfast he put on his Ssss…snow [everyone says *snow*] suit and ran outside. The ssss…[everyone says *snow*] was piled up very high along the street to make a path for walking."

When Ms. King and the children finish reading the book, she asks the children what they remember that Peter did in the story. Jovanna says, "He made angels." Jack says, "He climbed up a mountain of snow." Brad says, "He made a snowman."

Ms. King asks the children what they have done in the snow that Peter did. One child says she goes sleigh riding, another says he has snowball fights, and still another says she likes to make footprints like Peter did. Juan leans over to Ms. King and whispers, "Can I have that book to take home and read?"

Because there was so much interest in snow, Ms. King brings out her collection of books about snow—which includes *Snowballs* by Lois Ehlert (2000), a book of poems by Jack Prelutsky (2006) titled *It's Snowing! It's Snowing! Winter Poems*, and *Owl Moon* by Jane Yolen (2007)—as an introduction to learning about snow.

* * * * * * * * * * * * * * *

Young children deserve a rich supply of the very best literature because good stories challenge their intellect, inspire their imagination, help them make sense of the world, and nurture their desire to read (Fisher, Flood, & Lapp, 1999). By reading to children, teachers help them develop a personal relationship with books. Sharing literature with young children "educates the imagination, provides **language** models, and molds the intellect" (Cullinan, 1987, p. 6). After a teacher finishes reading a book aloud, it is not uncommon for children to want to explore the book on their own—to examine the pictures, retell the story as they turn the pages, and engage in pretend-reading. When children hear a good story, they often look for other books on the same subject or other books by the same author. Reading aloud to children can inspire them to want to read.

When a teacher reads aloud a good piece of children's literature, children are exposed to much more than an oral rendition of a storybook. The interaction that surrounds the storybook reading expands the language of the text (Sulzby & Teale, 1987).

> When a teacher reads aloud a good piece of children's literature, children are exposed to much more than an oral rendition of a storybook. The interaction that surrounds the storybook reading expands the language of the text.

During the conversation that occurs during storybook reading, children seek to understand the text. This construction of meaning may account for the powerful influence the exposure to children's literature has on literacy development.

Children's Literature and the Social, Emotional, and Intellectual Development of Young Children

Social Development

Socialization is the process of acquiring the beliefs, values, and behaviors that are valued and considered appropriate by older members of a society or community (Shaffer, 1989). Young children's social development is influenced by their observations of others and identification with role models (Norton, 1999).

When children receive encouragement or constructive criticism from adults, it reinforces socially acceptable behaviors and attitudes and discourages unacceptable ones. For example, a teacher might offer a warm response to a child who says something positive about another child or discuss inappropriate behavior with a child who says something hurtful to a peer. Children's literature can be used to help model appropriate or inappropriate social behavior and the resulting rewards and consequences (see Table 1 for recommendations). For example, in the book *Where the Wild Things Are* (Sendak, 1991), Max, the main character, behaves badly and his mother sends him to his room. He dreams about the kind of wild things his

---

Table 1
Recommended Books for Modeling Social Behavior

Adoff, A. (2004). *Black is brown is tan*. New York: Harper & Row.
Alexander, M. (2006). *Nobody asked me if I wanted a baby sister*. New York: Dial.
Hoban, R. (1994). *Best friends for Frances*. New York: HarperCollins.
Lionni, L. (1996). *It's mine!* New York: Random House.
Llewellyn, C. (2005). *Why should I share?* New York: Barron's Educational Series.
Miller, R. (2002). *The bear on the bed*. Toronto, ON: Kids Can Press.
Sendak, M. (1991). *Where the wild things are*. New York: Harper & Row.
Shemin, C. (2006). *Families are forever*. New York: As Simple As That.
Steptoe, J. (1988). *Baby says*. New York: HarperCollins.
Zolotow, C. (1982). *The quarreling book*. New York: Harper & Row.

mother said he was. When Max wakes up at the end of the story, his dinner is waiting for him. He realizes that in spite of his bad behavior he is still loved. Recognizing that he is loved points out that it is the behavior that is unacceptable—not him—and he is not likely to behave this way again.

Emotional Development

Teachers can use children's literature as a vehicle for fostering the development of healthy emotional attitudes. Literature contributes to the emotional development of children in three important ways:

1. Literature shows children that many of the feelings they experience are the same as those of other children.

2. Literature explores feelings from several viewpoints.

3. The actions of various characters illustrate options for different ways of dealing with emotions (Glazer, 1991). Literature can help children through difficult experiences such as death, divorce, loss of a friend, or hospitalization. In addition, literature can play an important role in helping children develop positive self-concepts.

All children face challenges in everyday life. Characters in children's literature can help children understand their own feelings and gain insights into how others have coped with similar problems (Norton, 1999). Read-aloud books such as those in Table 2 promote discussion and reflection as they support children's emotional growth.

Table 2
Recommended Books for Supporting Children's Emotional Growth

Aliki. (1986). *Feelings*. New York: Harper Collins.
Bang, M. (1999). *When Sophie gets angry, really, really angry*. New York: Scholastic.
Bourgeois, P. (2004). *Franklin says "I love you"*. Toronto, ON: Kids Can Press.
Bunting, E. (1989). *The Wednesday surprise*. New York: Clarion.
Cutler, J. (2002). *Darcy and Gran don't like babies*. New York: Farrar, Straus and Giroux.
Engel, D. (1999). *Josephina hates her name*. New York: Feminist Press.
Krauss, R. (1989). *The carrot seed*. New York: Harper.
McBratney, S. (2005). *Guess how much I love you?* Cambridge, MA: Candlewick.
Sharmat, M. (1993). *A big fat enormous lie*. New York: Puffin.
Steig, W. (1991). *Spinky sulks*. New York: Farrar, Straus and Giroux.
Tompert, A. (1992). *Will you come back for me?* Chicago: Albert Whitman.

Table 3
Recommended Books for Promoting Children's Intellectual Development

Cognitive Skill	Book
Observing	Selsam, M., & Hunt, J. (1989). *Keep looking!* New York: Macmillan.
Comparing	Jenkins, S. (1996). *Big & little.* Boston: Houghton Mifflin.
Classifying	Carle, E. (2005). *My very first book of colors.* New York: Crowell.
Organizing	Silverhardt, L. (2003). *I can get dressed!* New York: Simon & Schuster.
Summarizing	Galdone, P. (1983). *The gingerbread man.* New York: Clarion.
Evaluating	Rathmann, P. (2006). *Ruby the copycat.* New York: Scholastic.

Intellectual Development

Intellectual development refers to the changes that occur in children's cognitive skills and abilities over time. Children's literature supports intellectual development by encouraging the exchange of ideas and the development of thinking skills, including observing, comparing, classifying, organizing, summarizing, and evaluating. The type of book that is read aloud influences the nature of the discussion that follows. Picture books and alphabet books, for example, lend themselves to routine dialogue cycles (Sulzby & Teale, 1987). In a comparison of the talk initiated by children after read-aloud experiences, it was found that children generated more talk after listening to informational books than they did after listening to narrative texts (Pellegrini, Perlmutter, Galda, & Brody, 1990). See Table 3 for a list of books that promote the development of cognitive skills in young children.

> Children's literature supports intellectual development by encouraging the exchange of ideas and the development of thinking skills, including observing, comparing, classifying, organizing, summarizing, and evaluating.

Developing Literacy Skills Using Children's Literature

Reading aloud to young children has long been acknowledged as a critical aspect of early literacy development. According to the National Institute of Education, "the single most important activity for building the knowledge required for eventual success in reading is reading aloud to children" (Anderson, Hiebert, Scott, & Wilkinson, 1985, p. 23). When the teacher reads aloud, children have the opportunity to hear the rhythm, flow, and variety of book language. The benefits for children who are read to in preschool include increased **vocabulary**, complex language, improved

comprehension skills, and success in beginning reading (Cosgrove, 1989; Cullinan, 1992; Elley, 1989).

There is a strong relationship between storybook reading in the home and beginning literacy development (Teale & Sulzby, 1986). Early readers often come from homes where they were read to frequently from the time they were only months old (Clark, 1984; Morrow, 1983; Teale, 1981). While many children come from homes rich in literacy events, we know that some children, especially those from economically disadvantaged communities, have less exposure to literacy. Most educators agree that the preschool years are an especially critical time for providing rich literacy experiences for all young children.

Preschool teachers need to take advantage of teachable moments as did Ms. King in the vignette at the beginning of the chapter. They also need to be explicit in their teaching. We can't leave literacy development to chance in preschool, and we must be explicit about what we are teaching. When teaching literacy skills, teachers need to follow a structured framework. The following framework may be applied to any of the skills introduced in this book:

1. Explain the skill that is being taught to the children.

2. Model how to put the skill into practice.

3. Provide **scaffolding** for children through guided practice: Offer assistance if needed as children try to accomplish the task.

4. Provide time for children to practice the skill independently and to apply it in different contexts.

In the following example, we demonstrate how to apply the basic framework to teach children about story sequence.

Teaching Story Sequence

1. Explain the skill that is being taught to the children. The teacher might say, "After I read *The Three Little Pigs* (Galdone, 1984), I want you to remember the sequence in which the pigs' houses appear. Which house was built first, second, and third—the brick house, the straw house, or the twig house? Now I'm going to ask you to try and remember the kind of house that was first that the first pig had, the kind of house that was second that the second pig had, and the kind of house that was third that the third pig had. As I read the story, it will tell you the kind of house each pig had. I will put the felt figures of the houses on the flannelboard for you to see."

2. Model how to put the skill into practice. The teacher uses felt flannelboard figures as storytelling props. When she reads about the straw house of the first pig, she puts the figure of the straw house on the flannelboard. She does the same for the stick house of the second pig and the brick house of the third pig. After reading, she numbers the houses 1, 2, and 3 as a visual reminder of the story sequence.

3. Provide scaffolding for children through guided practice: Offer assistance if needed as children try to accomplish the task. The teacher assigns the children to work in pairs and gives each pair three paper houses that resemble the three felt houses. She asks the children to retell the story collaboratively and to arrange the houses on the table in front of them in the right order as they tell the story.

4. Provide time for children to practice the skill independently and to apply it in different contexts. During literacy center time, children can use the felt figures and flannelboard to retell the story of *The Three Little Pigs* and arrange the houses in the correct order. This thorough presentation with explicit instruction, guided practice, and independent practice provides a well-rounded plan.

Using Children's Literature
With English-Language Learners

One out of every seven children in U.S. classrooms is an **English-language learner** (ELL), a child whose first language is not English (Miramontes, Nadeau, & Commins, 1997). This number increases daily. We need to acknowledge diversity by being sensitive toward cultural and language differences.

To support ELLs, make sure that your classroom library includes books in their native language, English-language translations of stories from their country of birth, and informational books about a variety of cultures. Learn about the cultures represented in your classroom and learn a few words in each ELL's home language. Using some key phrases and sharing books related to an ELL's background will make the child feel welcome and comfortable in your classroom.

Preschoolers are likely to acquire English simply through immersion in an English-speaking classroom, something that older children cannot do. But it is important that they hear their own language as well. If possible, assign a bilingual child, one who speaks English and the language of the ELL, as a buddy. This child can help the ELL to understand classroom activities.

To help ELLs understand English, speak slowly, using simple language. Repeat phrases you want them to learn and use gestures and visual references when communicating (Shore, 2001). Helpful gestures such as motioning to sit down, stand up, or quiet down will help with communication. Teach ELLs functional language that will enable them to participate in classroom activities. Language that identifies cubbies for storage or names of centers in which to work are useful functional words.

For each ELL, make a book filled with photos or drawings of different parts of the classroom, such as the block center. Illustrate predictable daily routines to help make the child feel safe and confident in the classroom. In addition to this functional book, make books about topics of interest to children. For instance, you might make a book of fruit, with one picture and label per page. High-interest picture books and books with predictable patterns are particularly useful in helping ELLs learn English. Revisit the same books often with your ELLs to familiarize them with language structures. **Dramatic play** and storytelling props are useful tools for visually representing language.

Activities and strategies designed for ELLs will benefit most of the children in your class—they are simply effective early childhood teaching methods. The following activities are particularly helpful for ELLs:

- Reading to children and showing the illustrations
- Discussing stories that have been read aloud
- **Repeated reading** of stories
- Use of Big Books
- Small-group and one-on-one read-alouds
- Story **retelling**
- Partner reading (children read with peers)
- Buddy reading (children read with more experienced partners)
- Choral reading
- **Echo reading**
- Tape-assisted reading

- Integrating storybooks into content areas, such as art, music, and dramatic play
- Independent reading
- Independent use of story props for retelling stories
- Family storybook reading

You will learn more about these techniques as you read about them throughout this book. In addition, you may wish to refer to the list of culturally diverse children's literature in Appendix A.

Organization of This Book

This book explores the *why* and *how* of using children's literature in preschool. Chapter 2 demonstrates how to design a literacy center that enriches the classroom literacy environment and discusses how to read and tell stories to children. In this chapter, we describe the types and quantities of books and other materials needed for an effective literacy center and offer suggestions for helping preschool children take full advantage of these classroom resources.

Chapter 3 presents strategies for helping preschoolers comprehend stories and understand how books work. Even very young children can discuss and analyze literature. This chapter offers a variety of approaches for helping children understand and respond to both narrative and informational stories.

Chapter 4 discusses the use of children's literature in thematic instruction and in content areas such as dramatic play, art, music, social studies, science, math, and literacy.

Chapter 5 emphasizes the importance of sharing children's literature within families and suggests activities that parents and other caregivers can share with children at home and in school.

Appendix A includes a bibliography of different genres of children's literature that are recommended for preschool children. Appendix B provides a list of what is commonly being referred to as new literacies—reading matter that comes in a format other than a traditional print book, such as websites and television programs. Appendix C includes some additional storytelling techniques to use in the classroom.

All teacher and student names used in this book are pseudonyms. Descriptions of students and teachers are composite sketches that represent real classroom situations that we have encountered in our studies.

Think about and discuss your first positive memories of a literacy experience related to a particular book. Was it a parent who read to you? Was it a teacher? Why is the experience memorable? What emotions did it evoke?

Think about how you could use a particular book to help a child solve his or her own social, emotional, or physical problem—or problems of this nature that someone else is having. Carry out the idea with children and discuss the results.

Also think about how literature can help ELLs. Try reading a book that you believe will be useful with ELL students and discuss the results with your peers.

CHAPTER 2

Creating Literacy Centers for Reading, Storytelling, and Comprehending Books

Children's literature can motivate preschoolers to want to read. Children's experiences with books before and during preschool set the foundation for their literacy development in the years that follow. Preschoolers should be provided with a literacy-rich environment that offers choices of reading materials that are challenging and bring success. In a literacy-rich environment, many of the following activities take place:

1. Teachers model how to read books for pleasure and for information.

2. Children have opportunities to use books both independently and in social settings.

3. Children have opportunities to listen to stories read by their teachers, parents, and peers in a pleasant, relaxed atmosphere.

4. Teachers allow for response to literature through discussion, role-playing, and puppetry.

5. Children are able to take books home from the classroom literacy center.

6. Children experience varied genres of children's literature.

Storybook Reading Practices in Preschool

As stated in Chapter 1, the most important thing we can do to promote literacy development is to read to children. Being read to helps children develop positive attitudes toward reading. The ritual of reading promotes sharing; the warm feelings that are generated by a storybook reading remain long after the story ends. Some stories take on a special meaning as they become favorites between an adult and a child.

The experience must be pleasant and interactive to be beneficial. It is important to establish a relaxed atmosphere and to designate a special location for read-alouds. A rocking chair is a perfect spot for sharing books.

You may wish to let children take turns sitting near you in the rocking chair during storytime, with the other children in a single or double semi-circle. Because children enjoy seeing illustrations during story reading, hold the book so that it faces the group or pause periodically and turn the book so its pictures can be seen.

A story reading is like a dramatic presentation. Before reading a story to children, practice reading it aloud to yourself. Be expressive when you read a book to children. Match your voice and facial expressions to the character who is speaking. Read slowly and with a great deal of animation. Record or videotape your readings so you can evaluate and improve your technique. Begin each story with an introduction and set a purpose for reading to enhance comprehension, as shown in this example.

· · · · · · · · · · · · · · · ·

"Today I'm going to read a book about a little boy who has a new baby in the house. Now he has to share his things, which he never had to do before. The name of the book is *Peter's Chair*. The author is Ezra Jack Keats [1998]. While I read the story, think about the part of the story you like best. If you have a younger brother or sister, think about some of the ways in which your family is similar to Peter's."

· · · · · · · · · · · · · · · ·

When you have finished reading the book, begin a discussion with questions such as, "What part of the story did you like best? Who has a brother or sister?" "Have you ever had any problems with your brother, sister or a friend? What happened? How did you solve the problem?" These questions reflect the purpose stated at the beginning of the reading and enhance comprehension.

Interest heightens when stories are discussed both before and after reading, especially if they are related to issues that reflect children's real-life experiences or current school topics. Storybook reading activities offer an ideal opportunity to help children develop comprehension skills. This is illustrated in the following interactive story discussion, in which Ms. Elizabeth, a preschool teacher, leads a discussion with 4-year-olds after reading *Peter and the Wolf* (Prokofiev, 2008).

Ms. Elizabeth:	Which characters were good and which were bad?
Jazmin:	The wolf was bad, but everyone else was good.
Ms. Elizabeth:	Why do you think that?
Jazmin:	Well, the wolf wanted to eat the bird and the duck.
Tyrone:	No, that's not right. The wolf wasn't really bad; he was just hungry.
Marianna:	If he had food he wouldn't want to eat them. So they took him to the zoo so he could get food.
Ms. Elizabeth:	Was there anyone else bad in the story or who didn't do something right?
Students:	[in unison] NO!
Eva:	Well Peter's grandfather didn't want him to go into the woods alone, and he did. He didn't listen.
Ms. Elizabeth:	Why do you think the grandfather didn't want him to go into the woods alone?
Jovanna:	Well in the woods, even if an animal isn't bad, when it is hungry, it doesn't know anything else to do but eat something. So if there are wild animals around, children shouldn't go alone.
Ms. Elizabeth:	So was Peter good or bad?
Darren:	Well he wasn't really a bad boy, but he didn't listen and he almost got into a lot of trouble.
Ms. Elizabeth:	Even though it turned out okay, this story has an important lesson. We need to listen to parents, grandparents, or other grownups who know about danger so we don't get hurt. Did anyone ever do something they were told not to do?

Students:	[in unison] No.
Ms. Elizabeth:	Are you sure?
Sara:	I did. My mommy told me to sit down to drink my milk and hold my cup up so the milk wouldn't spill. I didn't listen and walked around with my milk and I didn't pay attention and it went all over the place. Splat! It made a mess. She didn't get mad; she just said I had to help her clean it up. It was hard work.

• • • • • • • • • • • • • •

Interactive discussions as a result of storybook reading generate problem solving, critical thinking, and positive and negative emotions in preschool children.

The Literacy Center

Children in classrooms with classroom literacy centers read and look at books much more often than children in classrooms without such collections. The efforts spent in creating an inviting atmosphere for a classroom literacy center are rewarded by increased interest in books (Guthrie, 2002).

Physical Space in the Literacy Center

The physical features of a classroom literacy center can play an important role in motivating children to use that area. Well-designed classroom literacy centers significantly increase the number of children who choose to participate in literature activities during free-choice periods. Conversely, in classrooms where the classroom literacy center is poorly designed, literature activities are among the least popular choices during free-choice periods (Morrow, 1982, 1987).

The classroom literacy center should be a focal area in a preschool classroom, immediately visible and inviting to anyone entering the room. However, many children crave privacy; sometimes they will look at a book in a coat closet or under a shelf. To provide some solitude, the center can be partitioned on two sides with bookshelves, a piano, file cabinets, or freestanding bulletin boards. Children can listen to recorded books with headsets to get a break from the commotion of the classroom. Alternatively, children can use a painted appliance carton as a cozy reading nook.

The dimensions of the literacy center will vary with the size of the classroom. Generally, it should be large enough to accommodate five or six children comfortably. Figure 1 illustrates the design of an effective preschool literacy center.

Because much of the activity in the literacy center takes place on the floor, the addition of an area rug and pillows or beanbag chairs makes the floor area more inviting. If possible, include a small table and chairs where children can use headsets to listen to taped stories. Designate an adult-size rocking chair as the Chair of Honor. Adults can sit in this chair to read to children, and pairs of children can sit there to read together. Invited guests can use this chair to present information to the class.

Soft elements, such as stuffed animals, belong in the literacy center, especially if they are related to books available in the classroom library. For instance, a stuffed rabbit might accompany *The Tale of Peter Rabbit* (Potter, 2006). Children enjoy reading to stuffed animals or simply holding them as they look at books. In addition, attractive posters that encourage reading are available from the Children's Book Council (www.cbcbooks.org) and the American Library Association (www.ala.org).

The Author's Spot is an integral part of the literacy center. It usually consists of a table and chairs and an assortment of writing materials. There are colored felt-tip pens, crayons, and lined white paper ranging in size. There may be a computer in the Author's Spot. The teacher can have some ready-made blank books for children to write in by stapling some white paper together adding colored construction paper covers. The books can be cut into theme-related shapes; for instance, use fish-shaped books for an ocean theme or butterfly-shaped books for a nature theme (see Figure 2).

The Library Corner

The library corner is one part of the literacy center. In a well-designed library corner, books are stored in several ways. Some books are shelved with the spines facing out. Some are on open-faced bookshelves, with the covers visible, which allows children easy access. This arrangement helps call attention to featured books, which are changed regularly. An alternative to open-faced shelving is the circular wire rack, commonly found in bookstores. These racks and open-faced shelving are ideal for highlighting new selections and books that relate to the theme being studied.

Figure 1
The Classroom Literacy Center

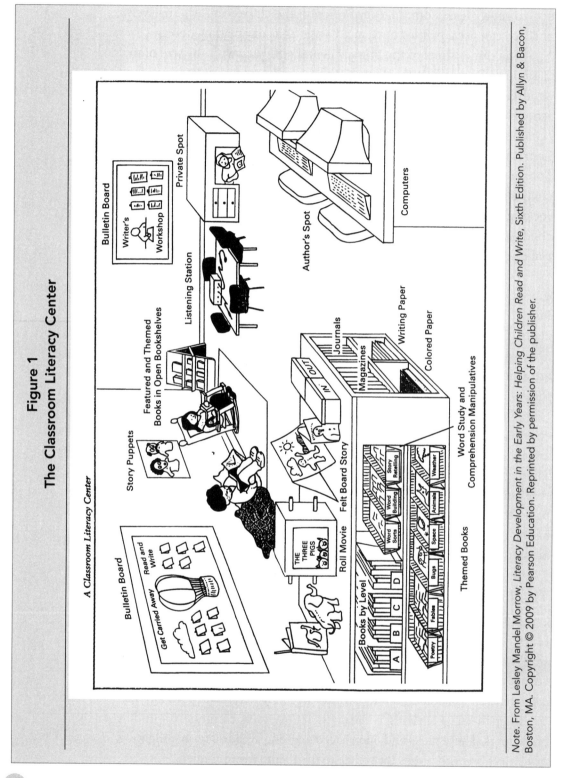

A Classroom Literacy Center

Note. From Lesley Mandel Morrow, Literacy Development in the Early Years: *Helping Children Read and Write*, Sixth Edition. Published by Allyn & Bacon, Boston, MA. Copyright © 2009 by Pearson Education. Reprinted by permission of the publisher.

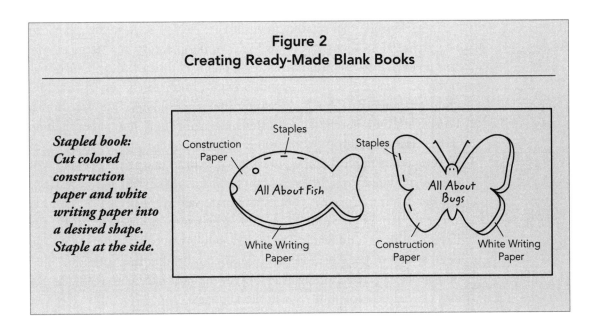

Figure 2
Creating Ready-Made Blank Books

Stapled book: Cut colored construction paper and white writing paper into a desired shape. Staple at the side.

Construction Paper

Staples

All About Fish

White Writing Paper

Staples

All About Bugs

Construction Paper

White Writing Paper

Books in the collection can be color-coded and shelved by category. Animal books, for example, might be identified with a blue dot on their spines and clustered on a shelf marked "Animals," with a blue dot next to the label. Another method is to store books by categories in plastic crates, with labels on the front of the crate indicating the types of books in the container. With preschool children, an illustrated label is helpful; for example, a picture of a plant with the word *plant* can accompany books on this topic.

How big should the classroom library collection be? A preschool classroom library should offer five to eight books per child, with books ranging across three to four levels of difficulty. It is advisable to stock multiple copies of some books. Children enjoy looking at the same book with a friend (Morrow, 1985). The collection should include narrative fiction and informational nonfiction (sometimes referred to as expository text). In the past, collections for early childhood were almost exclusively narrative stories. However, as adults, most of the material we read is non-fiction; for this reason, children need a lot of experience with informational text. Now educators have come to realize that informational, nonfiction books should comprise one-third to one-half of the total selections in a preschool classroom library (Moss, Leone, & Dipillo, 1997).

> A preschool classroom library should offer five to eight books per child, with books ranging across three to four levels of difficulty. It is advisable to stock multiple copies of some books. Children enjoy looking at the same book with a friend. The collection should include narrative fiction and informational nonfiction (sometimes referred to as expository text).

Books and other reading materials are easy to accumulate. They can be purchased inexpensively at yard sales or flea markets. Teachers can borrow up to 20 books a month from most public libraries, ask for book donations from parents, and hold fundraisers for book purchases. In addition, children's paperback book clubs offer inexpensive books and free bonus books with bulk purchases. Children's magazines and newspapers belong in the classroom library, too, even if they are not current. For the cost of mailing and shipping, some publishers and local magazine agencies will donate outdated periodicals to schools. To ensure continued interest, the teacher can introduce new books and materials in the library corner. We suggest introducing about 20 new books each month, replacing 20 that have been there for a while. The 20 new books can be selections that have been stored in the closet for a while. By continuing this rotation, "old" books will be greeted as new friends a few months later. Circulating books also can help compensate for a limited budget.

Establish a classroom system for children to check out the books. Preschool children need adult assistance to check out and return books. The checkout system should be simple, such as copying titles and recording dates on index cards filed under the child's names. Another method for checking out books is to use a loose-leaf notebook with a page for each child to record books taken out and returned. Figure 3 provides a sample page from a checkout notebook.

Figure 3
Notebook Page for Classroom Checkout System

Name: Juan Morales

Name of Book	Date Out	Date In
How Do Dinosaurs Eat Their Food?	March 7	March 11
Getting to Know Sharks	March 8	

Types of Books in the Library Corner

Books and other materials selected for the library corner should appeal to a variety of interests and span a range of levels. Preschoolers enjoy reading cloth books and board books, as well as hardback and paperback books.

Children particularly benefit from predictable literature. Predictability helps children understand the story line more easily and enables them to join in as the book is read aloud. Predictable literature features rhyme; repetition; catchphrases; familiar sequences, such as days of the week or numbers; cumulative patterns, in which events are repeated or added on as the story continues; stories about familiar topics; and familiar or popular stories.

Picture Storybooks.   When we think of children's literature, most often we think of picture storybooks, in which the text is closely associated with the illustrations. A good picture storybook will include a setting, theme, plot, and resolution. Picture storybooks are available on a wide range of topics, and many are known for their excellence. The Caldecott Medal is awarded annually to the illustrator of an outstanding picture storybook; any classroom library should include an assortment of Caldecott-winning books. For example, a very popular book with children is *Where the Wild Things Are* by Maurice Sendak, which was a Caldecott Medal winner in 1963 (see Appendix A).

Realistic literature is a subcategory of picture storybooks that deals with real-life issues. For preschool children, two common problems are bedtime fears and coping when a new baby joins the family. Other topics of interest might include visits to the doctor and the dentist.

Picture Concept Books.   Picture concept books are appropriate for the very young child. Most picture concept books do not have story lines, though they often have themes, such as animals or food. Each page usually includes a picture identified by a printed word. Many picture concept books are made of cardboard, cloth, or vinyl to withstand rigorous handling. Alphabet and number books also are considered picture concept books.

Traditional Literature.   Traditional literature includes nursery rhymes, folk tales, fairy tales, and other familiar stories that are part of our heritage and originated in the oral tradition of storytelling. We often assume that children are familiar with *Goldilocks and the Three Bears* (Brett, 1996) and

The Three Little Pigs (Galdone, 1984), yet many children have not been exposed to these traditional stories. Children who do know the stories welcome them as old friends. Folk tales are often retold in picture-book style. Many of these stories originate in other countries and cultures, and therefore broaden a child's experience and knowledge base.

Poetry. Poetry is too often forgotten in collections of children's literature. Many themed anthologies have been compiled for young children, and they should be an important part of the library corner.

Big Books. Big Books, oversized picture books that rest on an easel, allow groups of children to see the pictures and the print as it is being read. They may be either enlarged versions of books originally published in a different format, or books written specifically for the Big Book format. Big Books help young children to make the association between oral and written language and make it easy for teachers to demonstrate how print is read from left to right across the page.

Informational Books. As mentioned early in this chapter, informational books, or expository text, are nonfiction books. These books broaden children's background information, help them to explore new ideas, and often stimulate a deep interest in a particular topic. Quality expository text will follow a definitive structure such as description, sequence, compare and contrast, cause and effect, or problem and solution. Preschoolers generally enjoy books about topics such as communities, dinosaurs, and famous people. Informational texts for preschoolers also can include menus, signs, newspapers, greeting cards, recipes, and so on.

Surveys of early childhood classrooms show that expository text comprises a very small proportion—less than 15%—of the materials read aloud (Yopp & Yopp, 2000). The common belief has been that children should learn to read and listen to narrative text in the early childhood years and then progress to reading expository text to learn information in the elementary grades. However, this approach can cause difficulty for students when they enter fourth grade and are suddenly expected to read expository text but have little experience with the genre. It simply isn't true that 3- to 8-year-olds are too young to understand and enjoy expository books. When selecting books to read for your classroom, be sure to choose both expository and narrative text.

New Literacies.   The term *new literacies* recognizes unconventional print forms as types of reading materials for children to read. It also recognizes artifacts and experiences as the source for seeking out literacy materials to learn more. Computer-related technology provides the greatest source of new literacies. For example, you can find storybooks online to read to children, use the Internet for information, e-mail to compose letters to correspond with others, and discover websites to create a place for students' work to be posted, such as their responses to literature. Students can also find out more about their cultural heritage through Internet research. Refer to Appendix B for recommended children's websites and television programs.

The Importance of Quality

Whatever materials you select for your classroom, it is important to pay attention to quality. Good picture books include clear and uncluttered illustrations. Quality narrative texts feature the following characteristics:

- A vivid setting and well-delineated characters
- A well-designed theme concerning the problem or goal of the main character
- A series of episodes or plot points that help the main character to solve his or her problem or achieve the goal
- A resolution in which the problem is solved or the goal is achieved

Quality expository texts feature one or more of the following structures (Vukelich, Evans, & Albertson, 2003):

- Description: Gives the reader a picture of the subject based on story observation.
- Sequence: Explains the steps that produce a certain product or outcome.
- Comparison and Contrast: Comparisons are usually made in two ways. In block comparisons, two items with a similar classification are compared and then contrasted. In point-by-point comparisons, similarities and differences are compared alternately.
- Cause and Effect: Causality tells why something happens.
- Problem and Solution: A problem is presented, followed by its solution. An understanding of chronology is necessary to comprehend this structure.

- Exemplification (reason and example): The main idea is printed with supporting details.

Creative Storytelling in the Literacy Center

Storytelling has a power that reading aloud does not, for it frees the story-teller to use creative techniques. It also has the advantage of keeping the storyteller close to the audience. Telling a story produces an immediate response from children and is one of the surest ways to establish a rapport between the listeners and the storyteller. Long pieces of literature can be condensed for preschool audiences so that a story can be told in a single sitting. Considered an art, storytelling can be mastered by most people.

When telling a story, it is not necessary to memorize the words, but be sure you know the story well. Learn the catch-phrases and quotes that are important to the story. Using an expressive voice enlivens your presentation, but do not let your dramatic techniques overshadow the story itself. Look directly at the children and take their attention into consideration. Have the original book at hand when you have finished telling a story so that the children can enjoy the story again through pictures and printed text (Ritchie, James-Szanton, & Howes, 2002).

> Storytelling has a power that reading aloud does not, for it frees the storyteller to use creative techniques. It also has the advantage of keeping the storyteller close to the audience. Telling a story produces an immediate response from children and is one of the surest ways to establish a rapport between the listeners and the storyteller.

Creative Techniques

Creative techniques help storytelling come alive. They excite the imagination, involve the listeners, and motivate children to try storytelling themselves. Take clues for creative techniques from the story. Some stories are perfect for the flannelboard, others lend themselves to the use of puppets, and still others can be presented as chalk talks, stories told with drawings on the chalkboard.

Flannelboards.   Flannelboards with story characters are a popular and important tool in a classroom. You can purchase flannelboard story characters or make your own by drawing figures on construction paper and covering them with clear contact paper or laminate. Attach strips of felt or sandpaper to the backs of the cutouts so they cling to the flannelboard. Narrative and expository texts with a limited number of events and characters are best for flannelboard retelling. Figure 4a shows a child using a flannelboard to identify characters while "reading" a story, and Figure 4b shows children using images and words to tell a story.

Figure 4
Working With Flannelboard

4a. A student identifies story characters using flannelboard.

4b. Students collaborate to tell a story using flannelboard.

Puppets.   Puppets are used with stories rich in dialogue. There are many kinds of puppets, including finger, hand, stick, and face puppets. Shy children often feel secure telling stories with puppets. Stories such as *The Gingerbread Boy* (Galdone, 1983) and *The Little Red Hen* (Galdone, 2006) are ideal for retelling with puppets because they are short, have few characters, and repeat dialogue. Informational books also can be retold using a puppet. Figure 5 provides patterns for creating puppets, and Figure 6 shows children using puppets along with flannelboard characters in the literacy center.

Music and Sound Effects.   Music can be used to accompany almost any story. Music and sounds add interest to storytime. You and the children can use rhythm, voice, and musical instruments to provide sound effects for stories. When preparing to tell a story, first select those parts of the story for which sound effects will be used. Then decide on each sound to be made and who will make it. As the story is told, each person can chime in with his or her assigned sounds. Record the presentation, and then leave the recording in the literacy center with the original book for the children to listen to later. Books that work well with sound effects include *Too Much Noise* (McGovern, 1992) and *Mr. Brown Can Moo! Can You?* (Dr. Seuss, 1970).

Props.   To add a visual element to storytelling, collect stuffed animals, toys, and other articles that represent characters and objects in a story. Display the props at appropriate times during the storytelling. For example, three stuffed bears and a blonde-haired doll can be used as props for *Goldilocks and the Three Bears* (Brett, 1996) and several toy trains can be used as props for *The Little Engine That Could* (Piper, 2005).

Chalk Talks.   Chalk talks are another technique that attracts listeners. The storyteller draws the story while telling it. Chalk talks are most effective when done with a large chalkboard so that the entire story can be drawn in sequence from beginning to end. Stories also can be drawn on mural paper, using crayons or felt-tip markers instead of chalk. Choose a story with simple illustrations. Draw only a select few pictures as you tell the story. There are stories that have been written as chalk talks, such as *Harold and the Purple Crayon* (Johnson, 1981) and its sequels. An example of a chalk talk can be found in Appendix C.

Figure 5
Puppet Patterns

Directions: Make transparencies from the figures. Tape oaktag on the wall. Project the transparencies on an overhead projector onto the oaktag to get the size you want. Face patterns (with cutout ovals) should be large enough for students to stand in back of them and show their faces through the cutout portion. Draw the image and color it, adding special touches for specific stories. Cover with clear contact paper or laminate, and then cut out. Attach sandpaper to the back of puppets to adhere to flannelboard, or attach tongue depressors or Popsicle sticks to the back of puppets to create stick puppets.

(continued)

Figure 5 *(continued)*

Figure 6
Using Puppets in the Literacy Center

flannel board

Recorded Stories. Headsets with recorded stories enable children to listen to the story on the headset as they follow along in the text. They are helpful for ELLs because they provide a model for correct English and fluent reading. Have parents and other classroom volunteers make tape-recordings of favorite stories.

Electronic Storybooks. Some excellent children's books have been published in an electronic format. The text is read aloud as images move on the screen. Because these stories are animated, they are motivating to children and enhance early literacy skills. Another advantage of electronic books is that skill activities are embedded within storybook reading (Wepner & Ray, 2000). Electronic stories can be projected on a screen for the entire class or listened to alone or with a peer, independent of the teacher.

Children have a great deal of control over the electronic storybook. They can determine the pace of the story presentation and when the pages are turned. They can select a story to read and reread. The story can be programmed to be read word by word or line by line.

Children can interact with characters in the book by labeling illustrations, and words spoken by the child can immediately become animated text. Some software story programs allow children to change the story line as the story is being told. Other programs enable young children and adults to create their own books. These books can be personalized and include photos of family members, pets, the children's homes, and so on. They can include predictable and repetitive phrases so that young children can read their own books. A child might compose a story like the following about a pet:

> My dog likes his dog food.
> My dog likes people food.
> My dog likes to play.
> My dog likes me.

In addition to building literacy skills, reading electronic storybooks and creating personalized books helps children gain self-esteem as they choose among the many options in the software programs (McKenna, 2001). Some story samples with creative techniques can be found in Appendix C.

Modeling Storytelling Techniques

This list of storytelling techniques is far from exhaustive. You and the children will discover many other ways to tell stories. When you model storytelling strategies for children, they become motivated to tell stories themselves. After a storytelling session, children can tell the story you modeled with one of the techniques you used. Preschoolers will create stories spontaneously with a puppet or with flannelboard story figures.

Engaging in storytelling is an important experience for children. When children tell stories in a presentation manner, as they do with flannelboard story characters, they demonstrate their comprehension of the text. They talk about the details of a story, the main idea, the story events, and the resolution. They interpret voices of characters as they tell the story. In the following vignette, one author, Lesley, recalls a successful flannelboard activity from her preschool teaching experience.

When I taught preschool, I wanted the children to learn to use the flannelboard to tell and retell stories. I decided to model using the flannelboard by sharing an easily adaptable, highly predictable story with the class.

The name of the story was "A Bunny Named Pat," an anonymous tale about a gray bunny who does not like his color because it is so plain. Pat is able to change his color, but each time he does, he has an unpleasant adventure. The story features the following refrain: "I'm a bunny named Pat/I'm sassy and fat/and I can change my color, just like that."

When I introduced the story to the children, I asked them to listen for the different colors that Pat becomes and the problems he faces each time. I then told the story, using the different colored bunny characters on the flannelboard. When the story was over, we discussed Pat and his different colors. We also discussed the ending of the story and its meaning, trying to relate it to the experiences of the children. I asked children if they ever wanted to be anyone other than themselves, and if so, why.

After the discussion, I asked the children to think of another color that Pat could become and devise a new adventure for the bunny. The children could select a colored bunny from bunny figures of different colors, and then tell about Pat's new color and his adventure. The bunnies were all made of construction paper and had felt strips glued onto the back to make them stick to the flannelboard.

Four-year-old Lindsey shared her story:

"I'm a bunny named Pat, I'm sassy and fat, and I can change my color just like that." Pat made himself red like an apple. Some bees was coming. They saw Pat in the red color and they were thinking that Pat was an apple. The bees went near Pat, they wanted to eat him. Pat ran and ran but the bees went after him. So he said, "Being red is not so good, I'm a bunny called Pat, I am sassy and fat, and I can change my color, just like that."

This activity involved children in discussing and creating a story. The experience is motivating because it actively involves the children with the story. The theme of the story, self-image, is an important topic for conversation and can help children understand each other's strengths, weaknesses, and needs. Figure 7 presents instructions for sharing "A Bunny Named Pat" in the classroom, along with a Pat the Bunny flannelboard pattern.

Using the Literacy Center

As preschool educators, we hope to inspire children to become lifelong voluntary readers. When books are celebrated, young children are more likely to develop a positive attitude toward reading. In addition to read-alouds and other teacher-led activities, children need time to explore books and storytelling materials alone and with peers. With careful planning, teachers can help children make effective use of time and materials in the literacy center.

Independent Reading Time

Designate about 10 minutes each day for children to look at or read books in the literacy center. During this time, children can select books they'd like

---

Figure 7
Instructions for Sharing "A Bunny Named Pat"

Directions: Using the Pat the Bunny flannelboard pattern provided here, create five identical flannelboard characters each of a different color: gray, blue, yellow, green, and orange. As you tell the story below, hold up and place a new colored bunny on the flannelboard as each bunny is named. The children can retell the story with the felt characters on their own. They enjoy the repetition and demonstrate comprehension.

"A Bunny Named Pat" (An Anonymous Tale)
Once upon a time there was a little gray bunny and his name was Pat. One day he looked around and saw that all his brothers and sisters, cousins and friends were gray, too. He thought he would like to be different from them. So he said,
  "I'm a bunny called Pat, I'm sassy and fat,
  And I can change my color—just like that." (Snap fingers.)
  And suddenly Pat was a blue bunny. He was blue like the sky and blue like the sea. He was blue like the twilight and blue like the dawn. It felt nice and cool to be blue. He decided to take a look at himself in the pond. He hurried to the edge and admired his reflection in the water. He leaned over so far that...SPLASH! He fell into the pond. Pat fell deep into the blue water and he couldn't swim. He was frightened. He called for help. His friends heard him, but when they came to the pond they couldn't see him because he was blue just like the water. Fortunately a turtle swam by and helped Pat get safely to shore. Pat thanked the turtle. He decided that he didn't like being blue. So he said,

(continued)

Figure 7 *(continued)*

"I'm a bunny called Pat, I'm sassy and fat,
And I can change my color—just like that." (Snap fingers.)

And this time, what color did he change himself to? Yes, he was yellow—yellow like the sun, yellow like a daffodil, yellow like a canary bird. Yellow seemed like such a happy color to be. He was very proud of his new color, and he decided to take a walk through the jungle. Who do you think he met in the jungle? He met the lion and the tiger. The lion and the tiger looked at Pat's yellow fur and said, "What are you doing in that yellow coat? We are the only animals in this jungle that are supposed to be yellow." And they growled so fiercely that Pat the bunny was frightened and he ran all the way home. He said,

"I'm a bunny called Pat, I'm sassy and fat,
And I can change my color—just like that." (Snap fingers.)

And this time, what did he change his color to? Yes, he was green. He was green like the grass and the leaves of the trees. He was green like a grasshopper and like the meadow. As a green bunny, Pat thought he'd be the envy of all the other bunnies. He wanted to play with his other friends in the meadow. Since he was the color of the grass in the meadow, he could not be seen and his friends just ran and jumped about him, not seeing him at all or mistaking him for a grasshopper. So Pat the bunny had no one to play with while he was green. Being green wasn't much fun. So he said,

"I'm a bunny called Pat, I'm sassy and fat,
And I can change my color—just like that." (Snap fingers.)

And what color was he then? Right, he was orange. He was orange like a carrot, a sunset, orange like a pumpkin—he was the brightest color of all. He decided he would go out and play with all his brothers and sisters and friends. But what do you suppose happened? When his friends saw him, they all stopped playing and started to laugh, "Ha-ha, whoever heard of an orange bunny?" No one wanted to play with him. He didn't want to be orange anymore.
He didn't want to be a blue bunny because if he fell into the pond no one could see him to save him. He didn't want to be a yellow bunny and be frightened by the lion and the tiger. He didn't want to be a green bunny because then he was just like the meadow and none of his friends could see him. He said,

"I'm a bunny called Pat, I'm sassy and fat,
And I can change my color—just like that." (Snap fingers.)

Do you know what color Pat the bunny changed himself into this time? Yes, you're right. He changed himself back to gray. And now that he was gray, all of his friends played with him. No one growled or laughed at him. He was gray like a rain cloud, gray like an elephant, gray like pussy willows. It felt warm and comfortable being gray. From that time on, Pat the bunny was always happy being gray, and he decided that it's really best being just what you are.

to look at and read alone or with a peer. (Figure 8 shows a child reading alone in the literacy center.) To help children become engaged in independent reading, offer an appealing selection of books on a special shelf, in a basket, or in a plastic crate. Limit the number of books to make the selection process quick and easy (Ritchie et al., 2002). If you have 16 children in your classroom, there should be no more than 25 books on the independent reading shelf. Provide books that relate to the current topic of study in your classroom. If children are learning about animals, for example, you might select animal books to place in the independent reading basket or on the independent reading shelf. Also include a few books that are already familiar to the children, such as those that have been read aloud by the teacher (Morrow, 1990, 1992; Morrow, O'Connor, & Smith, 1990). At the end of an independent reading period, invite a few children to tell about the books they looked at or read. By discussing books in this way, children begin to learn accountability. They discover that they need to think about what they are reading as they read.

Figure 8
Independent Reading in the Literacy Center

Literacy Center Time

Literacy center time enables children to choose from several activities involving books and related materials. It is a more active time than independent reading, when only quiet book reading takes place. Children can look at books and use story-related manipulative materials. Before any of these are used by children, the materials need to be modeled by the teacher. In the beginning, the teacher can assign activities for children; once they become familiar with the center materials, the children may select activities themselves. At the literacy center, children participate in reading and writing activities independently and practice important literacy skills. Teachers can alternate having independent reading and literacy center activity time each day. The center time should last for about 15 minutes.

The Teacher's Role During Independent Reading and Literacy Center Time

Besides preparing the literacy center environment, the teacher also plays an important role before and during independent reading and literacy center time. He or she models activities, helps children select and start using materials, and participates in the children's activities when they need assistance. One of the reasons for independent reading and literacy center time is to engage children in self-directed activities; these are important behaviors to learn.

Independent Reading and Literacy Center Time in Action

In the following example, Jean Lynch and her class of 4-year-olds are engaged in several different literacy center activities on the last day of school.

• • • • • • • • • • • •

Louis and Ramon are squeezed tightly into a rocking chair, sharing a book. Marcel, Patrick, and Roseangela snuggle under a shelf—a private spot filled with stuffed animals. They take turns with their pretend reading.

Tesha and Tiffany are on the floor with a flannelboard and character cutouts from *The Gingerbread Boy* (Galdone, 1983), alternately telling the story and manipulating the figures: "Run, run as fast as you can! You can't catch me, I'm the Gingerbread Man!"

Four children listen to tapes of *Pierre* (Sendak, 1991) on head-sets, each child holding a copy of the book and chanting along with the narrator, "I don't care, I don't care."

• • • • • • • • • • • • • • •

Reactions to Literacy Centers

A study (Morrow, 1992) was carried out in which preschool teachers and children were interviewed from classrooms where they had literacy centers and literacy center time. This was done to determine their attitudes toward having the centers and center time in their classrooms. Teachers commented that the designing of a space for the literacy center demonstrated to the children that books were important in their classroom. Teachers agreed that children were attracted to the area by the manipulative materials in the center, such as the flannelboard stories and puppets. They found that the rocking chair, rug, pillows, and stuffed animals made the center relaxing and comfortable for reading. One teacher remarked, "The literacy center became a place where children sat together and shared books. This social context provided a warm atmosphere. The children looked forward to their time there each day." A child commented, "I liked to snuggle on the pillows with a book." Another child commented, "I like to sit in the rocking chair and read." Still another said, "I like to take books home from school."

Evaluating Literacy Center Time

To continue the study, during literacy center time, teachers were asked to observe their class to notice which children needed help getting started on a task and what activities the children were choosing to participate in. Teachers recorded anecdotes of activities. They made audiotapes and videotapes of the groups at work. Teachers discussed literacy center designs and how they might be improved to increase student productivity. They moved the center from one area of the room to another because they found a space that was bigger, brighter, or quieter. They added books and manipulatives to provide more choices for children. The evaluation form in Figure 9 provides a means for assessing your literacy center.

Assessing Children's Attitudes Toward Books

Observing children's behavior while they are listening to stories, reading, or looking at books is an effective method for assessing their attitudes toward books. How much attention do children give to the books they are looking at or reading? Do they simply browse? Do they flip through the pages quickly, paying little attention to print or pictures? Do they demonstrate sustained attention to pictures throughout the book (Martinez & Teale, 1988)? Note how frequently children choose to look at books when given a range of options. Use occasional one-on-one interviews to ask children what they like to do best in school and at home to determine their interest in reading. During parent–teacher conferences, ask parents if their children voluntarily look at books or pay close attention when they are read to. Also, ask parents how often they read to their children. Gather facts about the home literacy environment that will help you understand the child's attitude toward literacy activities. A checklist for assessing attitudes toward reading (see Figure 10) can be photocopied and placed in a child's **assessment** portfolio.

Young children are eager to learn and be introduced to new ideas. Books with nonfiction stories provide a wealth of information for children, who can have real and vicarious experiences through the stories.

PROFESSIONAL DEVELOPMENT FOR PRE- AND INSERVICE TEACHERS

Create a real or imagined space for a literacy center in your classroom. Make a sketch and list the materials needed. Take inventory of what you have and what you need. Figure out the cost to make it the type of center you would like it to be.

Make a list of the books you have in your classroom. Take stock of how many you have that are different genres and what you need to improve the collection. Make a list of books you want to add.

Visit classrooms of other teachers in your building to see what their literacy centers look like so you share ideas.

Read a story to your children or your peers during a study group to discuss the pros and cons of the presentation. Tell a story as a dramatization and critique each other. Tell a story with props.

Create a set of story puppets, props, felt figures, chalk talks, music, stories, etc., with your colleagues. Share these materials. Have parents come in and help to make some.

Evaluate your literacy center using Figure 9. Make changes based on what you find out. Evaluate a child's attitudes toward reading in Figure 10. Work with children in areas that need improvement.

Figure 9
Evaluating Your Literacy Center and Literacy Center Time

___ Children participate in some phase of the library corner design (develop rules, select a name for the area, develop materials, etc.).

___ The area is placed in a quiet section of the room.

___ The area is visually and physically accessible.

___ Part of the area is partitioned off from the rest of the room.

___ Bookshelves are available for storing books with spines facing outward.

___ Open-faced bookshelves are available for new or featured books.

___ There is an organizational system for shelving books (e.g., baskets by genre).

___ Five to eight books are available per child.

___ Many books are available representing three or four levels of difficulty and of the following types:

    __ picture storybooks

    __ traditional literature

    __ poetry

    __ realistic literature

    __ informational or expository texts

    __ biographies

    __ easy-to-read books

    __ riddle and joke books

    __ participation books

    __ series books

    __ textless books

    __ TV-related books

    __ brochures

    __ newspapers

    __ magazines

___ New books are circulated once a month.

___ There is a checkout system for children to take home books.

___ There is a rug.

___ There are throw pillows or beanbag chairs.

___ There is a rocking chair.

___ There are headsets and taped stories.

___ There are posters about reading.

___ There are stuffed animals.

___ The area is labeled with a name selected by the class.

___ There are a flannelboard and story characters, along with related books.

___ There are puppets and props for storytelling.

___ There are materials for writing stories and making them into books.

___ There is a private spot in the corner, such as a box to crawl into and read.

___ The area utilizes about 10% of the classroom; five or six children can fit easily.

Figure 10
Assessing Attitudes Toward Reading

Child's Name: _____ Date: _____

Voluntarily looks at or reads books at school.	Always	Sometimes	Never
Asks to be read to.	Always	Sometimes	Never
Listens attentively while being read to.	Always	Sometimes	Never
Responds during book discussions with questions and comments to stories read aloud.	Always	Sometimes	Never
Takes books home to read voluntarily.	Always	Sometimes	Never

Teacher Comments:

CHAPTER 3

Supporting Reading Comprehension: Responding to Books

• • • • • • • • • • • • • • •

Whenever Mrs. Johnson read aloud to the class, she began by naming the title, author, and illustrator of the book. She did this to encourage the children to look for the titles of books and the names of the
people who create them. One day, during literacy center time,
Damien placed *Chicken Soup With Rice* (Sendak, 1991) on the Big
Book stand. He gathered an audience of three children and began by
saying, "I'm going to read this book to you." Damien turned to the
first page and began pretend-reading the book to the children. Patrick
popped up and said, "Damien, you can't read the book yet; you forgot to read the title." Damien tapped his fist to his forehead, looked
somewhat annoyed with himself, and said, "How could I forget that?
The title of the book I'm going to read is *Chicken Soup With Rice*."

• • • • • • • • • • • • • • •

Damien and Patrick are demonstrating their knowledge of **concepts
of books**. Damien knows that books are for reading as he pretend
reads the story. He also knows that books have titles to be read
before the story begins.

Concepts of Books

Knowledge about concepts of books is an important milestone
on the road to literacy. Children with prior book experience may
already know some concepts about print such as how to handle
books, recognize the parts of a book, and recognize the difference between pictures and print. Other children will need to be
taught these concepts. A child who has a good concept of books

> Knowledge about concepts of books is an important milestone on the road to literacy.

- Knows that a book is for reading
- Can identify the front, back, top, and bottom of a book
- Can turn the pages of a book properly in the right direction
- Knows the difference between print and pictures
- Knows that pictures on a page are related to what the print says
- Knows where one begins reading on a page
- Knows what a title is
- Knows what an author is
- Knows what an illustrator is

Modeling Concepts of Books

We often assume that children understand basic book concepts. However, to many preschoolers, these concepts are totally unfamiliar. Therefore, teachers should read to children often and highlight book concepts at every opportunity. For example, you can introduce a story reading by pointing to the title of the book as you say, "The title of the story that I'm going to read is *Mr. Rabbit and the Lovely Present* [Zolotow, 1977]. This is the front of the book, and these words are the title."

On another day, you might explain, "The author of the book, the person who wrote it, is Charlotte Zolotow. Here is her name. And the illustrator, the person who drew the pictures, is Maurice Sendak. Here is his name."

Point out these concepts. Remind the children that all books have titles and authors, and if books have pictures, they also have illustrators or photographers. Discuss the difference between photographers and illustrators. After you have discussed these concepts, suggest to the children that they look for the title whenever they read a new book. Similar dialogue helps to explain other concepts. For example, when teaching children the difference between print and pictures, you could say, "Point to a picture; now point to the print. Which do we read, the picture or the print?"

Each time you read to children in whole groups, small groups, or individually, ask them to point to the top and bottom of the book and where you should begin reading on a page. This ritual reinforces important print concepts and helps you determine which children have a firm understanding of those concepts and which children need more instruction. With repeated practice, children begin to experience books in a new way. For example, after one 4-year-old had listened to *The Little Engine That Could* (Piper, 2005), she asked, "Show me where it says, 'I think I can, I think I can.' I want to see it in the book." When the teacher showed her the text, the child repeated each word while pointing to it and then asked to see the words in another part of the book. She proceeded to search through the rest of the book, reading with great enthusiasm each time she found the line, "I think I can, I think I can."

Using Big Books to Learn Concepts of Books

Big Books are an important part of early literacy instruction for children in preschool through the primary grades. The enlarged print and pictures in these books help introduce children to book concepts, print, and the meaning of text. When using Big Books in small- and large-group settings, encourage children to be actively involved. Position the Big Book so the children can see the pictures and text. You may want to place it on a stand for easier handling. You can purchase Big Books or make your own. Making Big Books in class helps children become even more aware of book concepts. Figure 11 provides directions for making a Big Book.

Big Books are effective for developing concepts about books because of their size. As the teacher reads the book and tracks the print from left to right across the page, children see that books are for reading. They notice where we begin to read on a page and learn to differentiate the print from the pictures. Children begin to realize that the reader's spoken words are being read from the print in the book.

In addition to learning concepts of books, children need to learn to understand what is read to them. Activities that ask them to respond to literature will help them learn to comprehend.

Developing Comprehension With Preschool Children

Comprehension, the ability to read or listen and understand text, is one of the major goals of reading instruction. When preschoolers listen to stories, comprehension can be an active process. Children rely on prior knowledge to interpret and construct meaning about what they listen to (Pressley & Hilden, 2002). Social interactions during reading enhance children's comprehension development (Teale, 1981). For example, children benefit from discussions with the adults who read to them.

> Comprehension, the ability to read or listen and understand text, is one of the major goals of reading instruction.

Figure 11
How to Make a Big Book

Materials

- 2 pieces of oaktag for the cover (14″ × 20″ to 20″ × 30″)
- 10 pieces or more of tagboard or newsprint the same size as the oaktag use for the cover to be used for the pages in the book
- 6 looseleaf rings (1¼″)
- Holepunch

Directions

- Punch three sets of holes in the top, middle, and bottom of the cover and in the paper that is to go inside of the book.
- Insert a looseleaf ring in each hole. The Big Book should have a minimum of 10 pages.
- Print should be 1½ to 2 inches high.

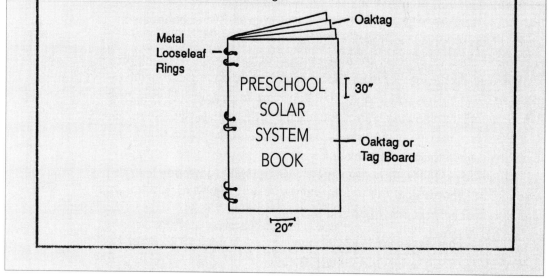

Reading and listening comprehension varies according to the difficulty of the text. Therefore, when reading to children, keep in mind the following text characteristics that will affect a child's level of comprehension (Graves, Juel, & Graves, 1998):

- The familiarity of the content
- The background knowledge required to understand the text
- How interesting the topic is to the listener

- The **syntactic complexity** of the sentences
- The amount and difficulty of vocabulary included
- The length of a selection

The RAND Reading Study Group report (2002) and the National Reading Panel report (National Institute of Child Health and Human Development [NICHD], 2000) both draw from research about successful comprehension practices to consider which comprehension strategies children need to learn and how these strategies should be taught. Although much of the discussion within these reports pertains to children who are in kindergarten through third grade and older, the following findings have great significance for preschool educators. Pressley and Afflerbach (1995) point out that to help young children learn to comprehend narrative and expository text, teachers need to

- Provide background information so that children have some prior knowledge of the text before it is read to them
- Ask children to anticipate and predict what might happen in a story
- Read materials to children from the beginning to end
- Refer back to the text to clarify any difficult parts
- Slow down when reading or listening to information that children need to remember and might be difficult for them
- Discuss the text with children after reading so they can reflect on ideas and summarize about what was read

The strategies that follow provide activities to engage preschoolers in learning to comprehend.

Developing Comprehension
With the Directed Listening–Thinking Activity

When children read or are read to, they need a purpose for reading or listening. The **Directed Listening–Thinking Activity (DLTA)** and **Directed Reading–Thinking Activity (DRTA)** strategies set a purpose for reading and listening and help to direct children's thinking. When teachers model these strategies through frequent use, children will internalize them and apply them when they read or listen to new material (Morrow, 1984; Stauffer, 1980).

Because this book deals with preschool education, we will focus on the DLTA. This strategy provides a framework for the listener for organizing and retrieving information. A DLTA can have many different objectives. The framework, however, is always the same: (1) preparation for listening or reading through questions and discussion, (2) reading the story with few interruptions, and (3) discussion after reading. All three steps focus on the DLTA's specific objectives. A DLTA can focus on literal responses (such as recall of facts and sequencing) and inferential responses (such as interpreting characters' feelings, predicting outcomes, and relating the story to real-life experiences). It can focus on identifying elements of story structure in both narrative and informational text. Research has demonstrated that a DLTA can increase the story comprehension of young listeners (Morrow, 1984), just as a DRTA can increase the story comprehension of young readers (Baumann, Seifert-Kessell, & Jones, 1992; Pearson, Roehler, Dole, & Duffy, 1992).

The following DLTA for *The Gingerbread Man* (McCafferty, 2001) develops two skills: Sequencing the events of a story and making predictions about the text.

1. Preparation for Listening or Reading Through Questions and Discussion.

It is crucial to build a background for what is going to be read to the children by introducing the story as follows: "Today I'm going to read a story called *The Gingerbread Man*. Let's look at the pictures and see if you can tell what the story is going to be about."

Encourage children to respond as you turn the pages of the book from beginning to end. This activity is sometimes called a **picture walk** (Fountas & Pinnell, 1996). After the children have offered their ideas say, "This story is about a little gingerbread man who escapes from the oven and all the people in the town try to chase him because they want to eat this delicious cookie. While I'm reading, try to imagine what will happen to the gingerbread man at the end of the story and why you think this. As I read, try to remember what happened first, second, third, and at the end of the story."

Ask questions that build additional background knowledge and set a purpose for listening. Relate the questions to real-life experiences whenever possible: "Have you ever tried to chase a friend but they got away? How do you catch someone when they are running away? Can you catch them without running after them? Do you have to be fast to catch someone?"

Once children are familiar with this questioning technique, you can ask them to think of their own questions: "Now that I've told you a little about the story, what did you want to find out when I read it to you?"

2. Reading the Story With Few Interruptions.   Be sure to show the children the pictures as you read the book. Stop only once or twice for reactions, comments, or questions. Don't interrupt the story for lots of discussion because discussion should occur after the story is read. Remind children to study the pictures. Model or scaffold responses to guide them in their thinking, keeping in mind the objectives for this particular DLTA. Some discussion questions for *The Gingerbread Man* could include the following: "Can you remember why the gingerbread man was running? Who was trying to catch him?"

If the children do not respond, model responses by changing questions to statements: "The gingerbread man was running so fast because everyone wanted to eat him. I remember when the cow tried to eat him." Children also can be asked to predict what will happen next.

3. Discussion After Reading.   The postreading discussion may be guided by the objectives or purpose set for listening to the story such as, "What happened to the gingerbread man first? Second?"

Ask children to retell the story to demonstrate their knowledge of sequence. Allow children to use the pictures in the book to help them recall the story sequence. Finally, focus on the second goal, making predictions, and ask, "Where do you think the gingerbread man would go next if he wasn't eaten by the fox? Do you think the fox and the gingerbread man could become friends? Why or why not? What do you think happened to all the people when they realized the gingerbread man had been eaten?"

Developing Comprehension With Shared Reading

Shared reading is usually carried out in a whole-class setting, although it may be carried out in small groups as well (Holdaway, 1979). During this activity, teachers model fluent reading for children and help them develop listening skills.

Sharing books enhances children's background knowledge, develops their sense of story structure, and familiarizes them with the language of books (Cullinan, 1992; Morrow, 1985). The language of books differs from oral language and provides a model for speaking. The following sentences from two well-known picture storybooks make this evident:

- "His scales were every shade of blue and green and purple, with sparkling silver scales among them." (Pfister, *The Rainbow Fish*, 1992)
- "I'm a troll from a deep dark hole, My belly's getting thinner; I need to eat—and goat's a treat—so I'll have you for my dinner." (Asbjornsen & Moe, *The Three Billy Goats Gruff*, 1991)

Shared reading often involves reading from a Big Book. Often the teacher uses a pointer while reading to emphasize the correspondence between spoken and written words and model the tracking of print. If the book is new to the class, the children should listen during the first reading. If the book is already familiar to the class, children should be encouraged to participate in the reading.

Children's participation in shared reading might include chanting story refrains, reading keywords, or stopping at predictable parts and filling in words and phrases. One popular technique is echo reading, where the teacher reads one line and the children repeat it. After the first reading, the Big Book and regular-size versions should be available for children to explore independently.

Shared book readings can be audio-recorded and made available in a section of the literacy center for listening. This provides children with a familiar model of fluent reading. They can emulate the teacher's phrasing and intonation as they "whisper read" along with the audio recording. Shared reading experiences can also be carried out using a DLTA format.

Using Predictable Texts/Stories. Predictable stories are ideal for shared reading experiences because they invite children to guess what will happen next. Predictability takes many forms. The use of catchphrases, such as "A house is a house for me" in *A House Is a House for Me* (Hoberman, 2007), encourages children to read along. Predictable rhyme, as in *Goodnight Moon* (Brown, 2005), makes it easy for children to fill in words.

Cumulative patterns contribute to predictability. New events are added with each episode, then repeated in the next, as in *Are You My Mother?* (Eastman, 2005). This book repeats phrases and episode patterns as its central character, a baby bird, searches for his mother by approaching different animals and asking the same question: "Are you my mother?"

Look for books that highlight familiar sequences, such as days of the week, months of the year, letters, and numbers, such as *The Very Hungry Caterpillar* (Carle, 1994). Conversation can also contribute to predictability, as in *The Three Billy Goats Gruff* (Asbjornsen & Moe, 1991) or *The Three Little Pigs* (Galdone, 1984).

Predictable books are excellent for young children who are just beginning to experiment with **emergent literacy** practices, as well as for conventional readers. They allow the child's first experience with reading to be enjoyable and successful with minimal effort. Such immediate success encourages the child to continue efforts at reading.

Repeated Reading.   When a story is read repeatedly, it becomes familiar and comfortable, like singing a well-known song. In addition to offering the pleasure of familiarity, repeated storybook readings help children develop concepts about words, print, and books. In a study with 4-year-olds (Morrow, 1987), one group listened to three repeated readings of the same story and the other group listened to three different stories. In an analysis of the discussions that followed the stories, the researchers found that during the course of the study, the responses of the children in the repeated reading group grew in number, variety, and complexity in comparison to the group that had a different story read to them each time. The children in the repeated reading group's responses became more interpretive and they began to predict outcomes and make associations, judgments, and elaborative comments. Children also began to narrate stories as the teacher read and to focus on elements of print, asking names of letters and words. Even children of low ability seemed to make more responses with repeated readings than with a single reading (Morrow, 1987; Pressley & Hilden, 2002).

Repeated readings promote independent reading; children can confidently revisit a familiar book without adult assistance. Children who are able to read independently or participate in pretend-reading behaviors often will select the same book to look at or read over and over again. Teachers can repeat readings of stories to children in a shared reading setting, encourage children to look at books more than once, and carry out discussions about books that have been read and discussed previously.

The following example of a 4-year-old child's responses to a third reading of *The Little Red Hen* highlights the child's comments and questions and the teacher's responses; most of the story text has been omitted.

• • • • • • • • • • • • • •

Teacher: Today I'm going to read a story called *The Little Red Hen*. It is about a hen who wanted some help when she baked some bread. [The teacher begins to read the story.] "Who will help me to cut this wheat?"

Melony:	"'Not I,' said the cat. 'Not I,' said the dog. 'Not I,' said the mouse."
Teacher:	That was good, Melony. You are reading. [The teacher continues reading.] "Who will take this wheat to the mill to be ground into flour?"
Melony:	"'Not I,' said the cat. 'Not I,' said the dog. 'Not I,' said the mouse with the whiskers."
Teacher:	Very nice, Melony. [The teacher continues to read.]
Melony:	I want to read that part, but I don't know how.
Teacher:	Go ahead and try. I bet you can. I'll help you: "The cat smelled it."
Melony:	[The child pretend reads parts she remembers from the repeated readings.] "The cat smelled it and she said 'umm that smells good,' and the mouse smelled it, and it smelled good."
Teacher:	[The teacher continues reading.] "Who will eat this cake?"
Melony:	"The mouse, the doggy, the kitty!"
Teacher:	You're right again, Melony. [The teacher reads to the end of the story.] Did you want to say anything else about the story?
Melony:	He was bad so he couldn't have no cake. [Melony searches through the pages.] That's the wrong part.
Teacher:	Show me the part you are talking about.
Melony:	There it is, almost at the end. She's going to make a cake and she'll say, "Who's going to bake this cake for me?" And the cat says, "Not I," the dog says, "Not I," the mouse says, "Not I." And then when she's cooking it they smell a good thing and then they wanted some, too, but they didn't have any, 'cause they didn't plant the wheat.
Teacher:	That's terrific, Melony.

(Morrow, 2005, pp. 171–172)

• • • • • • • • • • • • •

This type of sophisticated response can only happen when a child has heard a story repeated many times.

As adults we often tire of repetition; however, it has great value in early reading development. Sulzby (1985) observed children from ages 2 to 6 as they attempted to read favorite storybooks. Although they were not yet readers in the conventional sense, the children were asked, "Read me your book." Sulzby found that the speech children used in their "reading" was clearly different in structure and intonation from their typical conversations. They used vocabulary and syntax from the story. Children also demonstrated different developmental levels in children's oral "readings."

Figure 12 offers a classification scheme for children's emergent reading of favorite storybooks. To use this checklist, ask a child to read a story that is well known to him or her. Preschoolers will not read conventionally. However, from their attempts at storybook reading it is possible to observe characteristics of their emergent reading behavior.

Developing Comprehension With Small-Group and One-to-One Story Readings

The importance of reading to small groups and to individuals must not be overlooked. Too often considered impractical in school settings, one-to-one and small-group readings yield such tremendous benefits that they should be incorporated into preschool programs.

Small-group and one-to-one readings are effective in the preschool classroom because it is easier for preschoolers to pay attention to the teacher in settings with small numbers of children. One of the greatest benefits of one-to-one story reading is the interaction that results. Children gain a great deal of information from this close interaction, while adults discover what children know and what they want to learn.

> Small-group and one-to-one readings are effective in the preschool classroom because it is easier for preschoolers to pay attention to the teacher in settings with small numbers of children.

It has been found that one-to-one readings are especially beneficial for preschoolers who have had little experience with books at home (Morrow, 1988). When reading in small groups or in a one-to-one setting, it is important for teachers to encourage children to be interactive by asking them to respond to questions, discuss pictures in the book, and chant repeated phrases.

When teachers read to children frequently and initiate interactive discussions, the number and complexity of the children's responses increases.

Figure 12
Classification Scheme for Children's Emergent
Reading of Favorite Storybooks

---

1. **Attends to pictures but does not form oral stories**
   The child "reads" by labeling and commenting on the pictures in the book, but does not "weave a story" across the pages.

   yes____   no____

2. **Attends to pictures and forms oral stories**
   The child "reads" by following the pictures and "weaves a story" across the pages, using the wording and intonation of a storyteller. Often, however, the listener must see the pictures in order to understand the story the child is "reading."

   yes____   no____

3. **Attends to a mix of pictures, reading, and storytelling**
   The child "reads" by looking at the pictures. The majority of the child's "reading" fluctuates between the oral intonation of a storyteller and that of a reader.

   yes____   no____

4. **Attends to pictures and forms stories with characteristics of written language**
   The child "reads" by looking at the pictures. The child's speech sounds like reading, both in wording and intonation. The listener rarely needs to see the pictures in order to understand the story. With his or her eyes closed, the listener would think the child was reading print. The "reading" is similar to the story in print and sometimes follows it verbatim. There is some attention to print.

   yes____   no____

5. **Attends to print**
   a) The child reads the story, mostly by attending to print, but occasionally refers to pictures and reverts to storytelling.   yes____   no____
   b) The child reads in a conventional manner.   yes____   no____

Note. Adapted from Sulzby (1985).

Children offer many questions and comments that focus on meaning. Initially, they label illustrations; eventually they give more attention to details. Their comments and questions become interpretive and predictive and they draw from their own experiences. They also begin narrating— that is, "reading" or mouthing the story along with the teacher.

When involved in frequent small group or one-to-one storybook readings, children begin to focus on structural elements in a story, remarking on titles, settings, characters, and story events. After many readings, the children begin to focus on print, matching sounds and letters and reading words (Morrow, 1987). When children hear stories in small groups, they tend to respond more; they repeat one another's remarks and elaborate on what their peers have said. Table 4 provides guidelines for teacher interactive behavior during small-group and one-to-one story readings, and Figure 13 shows interactive behavior during a small-group story reading.

Productive discussions result from good questions. Good questions ask children to clarify information and predict outcomes. The following is a description of types of questions.

Literal questions ask students to

- Identify details such as who, what, when and where
- Classify ideas
- Sequence text
- Find the main idea

Table 4
Guidelines for Teacher Interactive Behavior During Small-Group and One-to-One Storybook Reading

Teacher Role	Specifics
Manage	• Introduce story. • Provide background information about the book. • Redirect irrelevant discussion back to the story.
Prompt Responses	• Children to ask questions or comment throughout the story when there are natural places to stop. • Model responses for children if they are not responding (e.g., "Those animals aren't very nice. They won't help the little red hen."). • Relate responses to real-life experiences (e.g., "I needed help when I was preparing a party, and my family shared the work. Did you ever ask for help and not get it? What happened?"). • When children do not respond, ask questions that require answers other than *yes* or *no* (e.g., "What would you have done if you were the little red hen and no one helped you bake the bread?").
Support and Inform	• Answer questions as they are asked. • React to comments. • Relate your responses to real-life experiences. • Provide positive reinforcement for children's responses.

Note. From Morrow (1988).

Figure 13
Interactive Behavior During Small-Group Reading

Inferential and *critical* questions ask students to

- Draw information from their background knowledge
- Relate text to life experiences
- Predict outcomes (What do you think will happen next?)
- Interpret text (Put yourself in the place of the characters)
- Compare and contrast
- Determine cause and effect
- Apply information
- Solve problems

Discussion questions should reflect children's interests and have many appropriate responses rather than just one correct answer. Questions with one correct answer can be asked occasionally, but the majority of questions should stimulate discussion and invite children to share their thoughts and feelings about the text. Include a few questions that deal with facts, main ideas, and story details. When asking questions, have children refer to the illustrations for possible answers. Once children are experienced at responding to questions, they can be encouraged to ask their own questions about a story that was read to them.

The following examples of small-group story readings in preschool illustrate the kinds of questions children ask and responses they make when they are engrossed in the reading experience. The examples reveal the rich information children receive from the adult reader and indicate what the children already know and what their interests are—useful information for anyone designing instruction.

· · · · · · · · · · · · · · ·

Story: *A Splendid Friend Indeed* (Bloom, 2007)—The child asks questions about book concepts.

Madeline: [points to the illustration on the book cover] Why does it have a picture on it?

Teacher: The cover of the book has a picture on it so you will know what the story is about. Look at the picture. Can you tell what the book might be about?

Jeanine: Ummm, I think it is about a big white furry bear and a duck and they like each other because they are smiling at each other.

Teacher: You're right, very good. The book is about a polar bear and a duck and they are good friends. The title of the book is *A Splendid Friend Indeed*. The pictures on the cover of a book and inside the book can help you figure out what the words say.

· · · · · · · · · · · · · · ·

Story: *A Splendid Friend Indeed* (Bloom, 2007)—The child asks for a definition.

Teacher: I'm going to read the story *A Splendid Friend Indeed*.

Jeannine: What is *splendid*?

Teacher: *Splendid* means wonderful, very good, terrific. Do you have a splendid friend?

Jeannine:	Devin is my best friend. I guess she is splendid. I will tell her.

Story: *Are You My Mother?* (Eastman, 2005)—The child attends to print.

Jordon:	Wait, stop reading. Let me see this again. [He looks at the page.] That says, "Are you my mother?"
Teacher:	You're right. Can you find it anywhere else?
Jordon:	I think so. Yes, here it is on this page. "Are you my mother?" And again over here, "Are you my mother?"
Teacher:	That is great, you are reading.

Story: *The Mitten* (Tresselt, 1989)—The child predicts.

Charlene:	I wonder if that mitten is going to break open?
Teacher:	Why do you think that?
Charlene:	Well, it is a mitten for a little boy so it isn't so big. All of those animals are going in it. Soon they won't fit.
Teacher:	Those are good ideas, Charlene. I'll read on and we will find out if you are right.

Story: *Knuffle Bunny* (Willems, 2004)—The child makes connections from one text to another.

James:	Hey this book is like the Mary Poppins DVD.
Teacher:	What do you mean?
James:	Well, you see the pictures in *Knuffle Bunny* in the back are real like real buildings and parks and stuff someone took those pictures with a camera of real things, and the pictures in the front are cartoons somebody drew. In the Mary Poppins DVD there are real people and then sometimes there are cartoon people and cartoon pictures, too.

Story: *Madeline's Rescue* (Bemelmans, 2000)—The child relates the text to real-life experience.

Jovannah:	What's the policeman going to do?

Teacher: He's going to help Madeline. Policemen are nice; they always help us.

Jovannah: Policemans aren't nice. See, my daddy beat up Dominic and the policeman came and took him away and put him in jail. And my Daddy cried and I cried. I don't like policemans. I don't think they are nice.

• • • • • • • • • • • • • • • •

These examples reveal children's understanding of text. The children's comments and questions relate to literal meanings; they raise interpretive and critical issues by associating the story with their own lives, predict what will happen next in a story, or express judgments about characters' actions. Their responses also relate to matters of print, such as names of letters, words, and sounds.

Analyzing one-to-one and small-group story readings reveals what children know and what they want to know about the texts that are read to them (Morrow, 1987). The coding sheet in Figure 14 will help in this analysis. The coding is a form of assessment-guided instruction that teachers can use to determine what the child knows and then decide what needs to be done to accommodate the children's needs when designing instruction.

Although whole-class readings are practical and effective in exposing children to literature, they do not promote the interaction between adults and children that takes place in one-to-one and small-group readings. If we review transcripts of story readings in all three settings, several things become apparent. In whole-group settings, children are discouraged from asking questions or commenting during the story because doing so interrupts the flow of the story for the rest of the audience. In this setting, the discussion has to be managed by the teacher to such an extent that he or she often talks more than the children do. Because of the size of the group, a truly interactive situation cannot exist. However, in small-group and one-to-one story readings, a teacher may manage and prompt the discussion at first, but only to encourage and model responses for children. The roles reverse in a short time, and soon most of the dialogue is initiated by the children (Morrow, 1987).

Children who do not experience one-to-one readings at home are at a disadvantage in their literacy development. By reading to a child individually

Figure 14
Coding Children's Responses During Story Readings

Directions: Read a story to one child or a small group of children. Encourage the children to respond with questions and comments. Record the session. Transcribe or listen to the recording, noting each child's responses by placing checks in the appropriate categories. A category may receive more than one check, and a single response may be credited to more than one category. Total the number of checks in each category.

Child's Name_____ Date_____

Name of Story_____

1. Focus on Story Structure
    ___ identifies setting (time, place)
    ___ identifies characters
    ___ identifies theme (problem or goal)
    ___ recalls plot episodes (events leading toward problem solution or goal attainment)
    ___ identifies resolution

2. Focus on Meaning
    ___ labels pictures
    ___ identifies details
    ___ interprets characters and events (makes associations, elaborations)
    ___ predicts events
    ___ draws from personal experience
    ___ seeks definitions of words
    ___ uses narrational behavior (recites parts of the book along with the teacher)

3. Focus on Print
    ___ asks questions or makes comments about letters
    ___ asks questions or makes comments about sounds
    ___ asks questions or makes comments about words
    ___ reads words
    ___ reads sentences

4. Focus on Illustrations
    ___ asks questions or makes comments about illustrations

Note. From Lesley Mandel Morrow, *Literacy Development in the Early Years: Helping Children Read and Write,* 6th Edition. Published by Allyn & Bacon, Boston, MA. Copyright © 2009 by Pearson Education. Reprinted by permission of the publisher.

in the classroom, the teacher can compensate for what is not provided at home. With frequent one-to-one reading, children gain both literacy skills and positive attitudes toward books; they learn to associate books with warmth and pleasure. Time limitations and class size make it difficult to provide one-to-one and small-group readings in school, but asking aides, volunteers, and older children to help can alleviate the problem.

Developing Comprehension With Story Retellings

Encouraging children to retell stories they have listened to or read helps them develop vocabulary, syntax, comprehension, and sense of story structure (Ritchie et al., 2002). Retelling allows for original thinking as children incorporate their own life experiences into their retelling (Gambrell, Pfeiffer, & Wilson, 1985). With practice in retelling, children come to assimilate the concept of narrative or expository text structure. They learn to introduce a narrative story with its beginning and its setting, theme, plot episodes, and resolution. They also learn to retell narrative text by focusing on a particular aspect such as story structure, cause and effect, or problem and solution. In retelling stories, children demonstrate their comprehension of story details and sequence. They also interpret the sounds and expressions of characters' voices. In retelling expository text, children review what they've learned and distinguish the main ideas from the supporting details.

Retelling is not an easy task for children, but with practice they improve quickly. Be sure to inform children before they listen to a story that they will be asked to retell it (Morrow, 1996). Further instructions depend on the purpose of the retelling. If the intent is to teach sequence, for instance, then children should be asked to think about what happened first, second, and so on. If the goal is to teach children to make inferences from the text, ask them to think of personal experiences that are similar to those that happened in the story. Props such as flannelboard characters or book illustrations can be used to help children retell. Pre- and postdiscussion of text helps to improve retelling ability, as does the teacher's modeling a retelling for children.

Retelling also allows adults to evaluate children's progress. When assessing a retelling, do not offer prompts beyond general ones such as "What happened next?" or "Can you think of anything else?" Retellings of narrative text reveal a child's sense of story structure, focusing mostly on literal recall, but they also reflect a child's inferential thinking. To assess the child's retelling for sense of story structure, first divide the events of the story into four categories—setting, theme, plot episodes, and resolution. Refer to the guidelines for story retelling (see Table 5), and use an outline of the text to record the number of ideas and details the child includes within each category in the retelling, regardless of their order. Credit the child for partial recall or for recounting the "gist" of an event (Pellegrini & Galda, 1982). Evaluate the child's sequencing ability by comparing the order of events in the child's retelling with the proper order of setting, theme, plot episodes, and resolution. The analysis indicates not only which elements the child includes or omits and how well the child

Table 5
Guidelines for Story Retelling

Teacher Role	Examples
1. Ask the child to retell the story.	"A little while ago, I read the story [name of story]. Would you tell the story as if you were telling it to a friend who has never heard it before?"
2. Use prompts only if needed.	• If the child has difficulty beginning the retelling, suggest beginning with "Once upon a time...." or "Once there was...." • If the child stops retelling before the end of the story, encourage continuation by asking, "What comes next?" or "Then what happened?" • If the child stops retelling and cannot continue with general prompts, ask a question that is relevant at the point in the story at which the child has paused. For example, "What was Jenny's problem in the story?"
3. When a child is unable to retell the story, or if the retelling lacks sequence and detail, prompt the retelling step by step.	• "Once upon a time...." or "Once there was...." • "Who was the story about?" • "When did the story happen? Day or night? Summer or winter?" • "Where did the story happen?" • "What was the main character's problem in the story?" • "How did he or she try to solve the problem? What did he or she do first? Second? Next?" • "How was the problem solved?" • "How did the story end?"

Note. From Morrow (1996).

sequences, but also where instruction might be focused. Comparing analyses of several retellings over a year will indicate the child's progress.

Outlining a story to reveal its structure, characters, and themes creates a framework for evaluating a child's retelling. The outline of *Franklin in the Dark* (Bourgeois, 1987) shown in Figure 15 is a typical example of a story outline (Morrow, 1996).

Transcribing a child's story retelling word for word provides teachers with the data they need for analysis. The following is an example of a 4-year-old child's retelling of *Franklin in the Dark*.

● ● ● ● ● ● ● ● ● ● ● ● ● ● ●

Teacher: What's the title of the story I read to you today?

Philip: I don't know.

Teacher: *Franklin in the Dark.*

Figure 15
***Franklin in the Dark* Story Outline**

Setting
a) Once upon a time there was a turtle named Franklin.
b) Characters: Franklin (main character), Franklin's mother, a bird, a duck, a lion, and a polar bear

Theme
Franklin is afraid to go into his shell because it is dark inside his shell.

Plot Episodes
First episode: Franklin decides to look for help to solve his problem.
Second episode: Franklin meets a duck and asks for help. The duck tells Franklin that he wears water wings because he is afraid of the water.
Third episode: Franklin meets a lion who wears ear muffs because he is afraid of his own roar.
Fourth episode: Franklin meets a bird who uses a parachute because he is afraid to fly.
Fifth episode: Franklin meets a polar bear who wears a hat, mittens, and a scarf because he doesn't like the cold.
Sixth episode: Franklin shares his experiences with his mother.

Resolution
a) Franklin and his mother put a nightlight in his shell.
b) Franklin is no longer afraid to go into his shell.

Philip: *Franklin in the Dark*. One time Franklin didn't want to go in his shell. He was too scared. But his Mama says there's nothing in there. But Franklin didn't want to go in the shell because he thought there was monsters in there. He didn't like to go in because he was scared. It was dark. At the end he went in, he turned on a little nightlight and went to sleep. That's it.

• • • • • • • • • • • • • • •

Retellings can be evaluated for many different comprehension tasks. The directions to students prior to retelling and the method of analysis should match the goal. Figure 16 provides an analysis form for evaluating a retelling. The teacher checks for elements a child includes and determines progress over time.

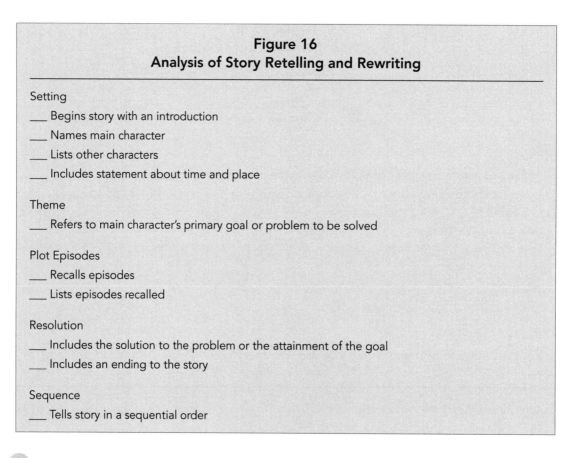

Figure 16
Analysis of Story Retelling and Rewriting

Setting
___ Begins story with an introduction
___ Names main character
___ Lists other characters
___ Includes statement about time and place

Theme
___ Refers to main character's primary goal or problem to be solved

Plot Episodes
___ Recalls episodes
___ Lists episodes recalled

Resolution
___ Includes the solution to the problem or the attainment of the goal
___ Includes an ending to the story

Sequence
___ Tells story in a sequential order

In his retelling, Philip names the main characters, Franklin and Franklin's mother. Philip restates the problem, the main character, and the theme. He understands the resolution of the story and his retelling has a clear ending. The parts of the story that Philip included are told in sequential order. However, Philip's retelling does not begin with an introduction. There is no statement of time and place. Aside from mentioning Franklin and his mother, Philip does not talk about any of the other four characters, nor does he recall any of the plot episodes in the story. From this evaluation, it is evident that Philip is able to recall the theme of the story, the resolution; future instruction should focus on recalling story details such as characters and plot episodes and beginning retellings with an introduction.

To illustrate progress over time, the following is a sample of a retell of *Jenny Learns a Lesson* (Fujikawa, 1980) by Philip at the end of the school year, eight months after the first retell (the first part of this example is an outline of the story, and the second part of the example is the student's retelling).

· · · · · · · · · · · · · ·

Story Outline

1. Once upon a time there was a girl who liked to play pretend.

2. Characters: Jenny (main character), Nicholas, Sam, Mei Su, and Shags, the dog.

Theme

Every time Jenny played with her friends, she bossed them.

Plot Episodes

First episode: Jenny decided to pretend to be a queen. She called her friends. They came to play. Jenny told them all what to do and was bossy. The friends became angry and left.

Second episode: Jenny decided to play dancer. She called her friends and they came to play. Jenny told them all what to do. The friends became angry and left.

Third episode: Jenny decided to play pirate. She called her friends and they came to play. Jenny told them all what to do. The friends became angry and left.

Fourth episode: Jenny decided to play duchess. She called her friends and they came to play. Jenny told them all what to do. The friends became angry and left.

Fifth episode: Jenny's friends refused to play with her because she was so bossy. Jenny became lonely and apologized to them for being bossy.

Resolution

1. The friends all played together, and each person did what he or she wanted to do.

2. They all had a wonderful day and were so tired that they fell asleep.

Student's Retelling

Once upon a time there's a girl named Jenny and she called her friends over and they played queen and went to the palace. They had to, they had to do what she said and they didn't like it so then they went home and said that was boring. It's not fun playing queen and doing what she says you have to. So they didn't play with her for seven days and she had she had an idea that she was being selfish, so she went to find her friends and said, I'm sorry I was so mean. And said, let's play pirate, and they played pirate and they went onto the ropes. Then they played that she was a fancy lady playing house. And they have tea. And they played what they wanted and they were happy. The end.

· · · · · · · · · · · · · ·

In this retelling of the story, Philip includes more characters, details, and episodes than he did in his first retelling, illustrating his progress in developing comprehension skills.

Developing Comprehension With Collaborative Strategies

The National Reading Panel report suggests that collaboration is an important strategy for developing comprehension (NICHD, 2000). Collaborative settings allow children to engage in productive conversations as they exchange ideas and learn to listen to each other. Teachers model the behaviors for collaborative activities before children participate in them with peers.

Collaborative settings allow children to engage in productive conversations as they exchange ideas and learn to listen to each other.

Buddy Reading.   Buddy reading involves pairing a child from an upper grade with a younger child. The child in the upper grade is instructed how to read to children. At specified times during the school week, buddies get together for storybook reading and discussions.

Partner Reading.   Partner reading involves peers reading together. This may simply mean that the children sit next to each other and share the same book. They take turns discussing the pictures or narrating the text.

Mental Imagery and Think-Alouds.   In mental imagery, children are asked to visualize what they see after they have been read to. Then, they are asked to conduct a **think-aloud**—to think aloud and talk about their images with peers and to predict what will happen next in the story. Children are encouraged to raise questions about the story and to look back at the pictures to recall forgotten details. They are also encouraged to personalize the text by relating their own experiences and actions to those in the story. Visualizing ideas and relating those visualizations orally to a peer helps young readers clarify information and increase understanding (Gambrell & Koskinen, 2002).

Fluency

The ultimate goal for reading instruction is that students be fluent readers. When a child is a fluent reader, he or she is able to automatically and accurately decode text and read with appropriate pace and expression, thus demonstrating comprehension (Kuhn & Stahl, 2003). Most preschoolers do not yet read conventionally, let alone fluently; however, even as listeners, they can participate in fluency activities. Fluency activities should be a daily part of the preschool curriculum. They are easy for teachers to plan, require little time, and are enjoyable for children (Rasinski, 1990).

Fluency is an underemphasized skill in literacy instruction. According to the National Reading Panel report (NICHD, 2000), helping children to become fluent readers is crucial for literacy development. Other researchers have found that echo reading, choral reading, and audio recording–assisted reading expose children to the rhythm, pace, and expression involved in fluent reading and are useful strategies for developing fluency (Kuhn & Stahl, 2003). For the preschool classroom, these strategies can easily be adapted to echo chanting, choral chanting, and audio recording–assisted listening.

Echo Chanting.   In echo reading, the teacher reads one line of text and the child then reads the same line. In echo chanting, children listen and then repeat what has been read to them. When reading to the children, be sure to model accuracy, pace, and expression. Try to echo chant a few times a week.

Choral Chanting.   In choral reading, the entire class, or a small group of children, reads a passage together. The teacher provides a model for pace and expression. Preschoolers who aren't yet conventional readers can chorally chant poems they have learned. In choral chanting, children experience the pace and expression necessary for fluent reading. Try to choral chant a few times a week.

Audio Recording–Assisted Listening.   Listening to fluent reading on audiotapes, CDs, or DVDs while following the pictures in a book provides an excellent model of reading for children. These recordings can be purchased or made by teachers, parents, and other students who are fluent readers.

Assessment of Concepts of Books and Comprehension

The techniques described in this chapter are designed to develop concepts about books and story comprehension through the use of expository and narrative text. The skills listed in Figure 17 for assessing concepts of books and comprehension of text can be used to check student progress. To determine how much children know about books, observe how they handle books. Have one-to-one interviews with children; encourage whole-group, small-group, or individual discussions. Children's story comprehension can be demonstrated and evaluated through their story retelling, attempted reading of favorite storybooks, role-playing, picture sequencing, use of puppets or flannelboards to reenact stories, and their questions and comments during storybook reading. When possible, keep periodic performance samples of activities, such as audio or video recordings of retellings.

Throughout this chapter, assessment tools for evaluating children's ability and needs have been provided. These materials can be placed in a child's portfolio or folder to evaluate his or her concepts of books, comprehension of text, and fluent chanting. Information about children's needs can be collected in September with assessment measures repeated a few times during the school year.

PROFESSIONAL DEVELOPMENT FOR PRE- AND INSERVICE TEACHERS

This chapter is filled with strategies to help your children comprehend. At a study group meeting have different teachers select a different strategy, such as one of the following:

- Conducting a story retelling
- Creating a DLTA
- Creating a shared reading lesson
- Doing repeated readings of the same story
- Reading to small groups of children to see the effect on discussion
- Engaging children in teacher-generated questions and helping them think of their own questions modeled after those the teacher asked

Reflect upon how the children responded and seemed to improve their comprehension. Each teacher needs to eventually try all the strategies and decide which they like best or what is best for which children.

In addition, if there is a coach in your building and you would like to see a strategy put into practice, it would be very helpful for you to observe a person who has used the strategy before using it with your children.

Teach your children to retell a story, first with the book or with props and then without. Use the prompts in this chapter to help the child with retelling. Have the children retell a story at three different times in the year. Fill out the story retelling form at each retelling and watch for progress, strengths, and weaknesses to teach to.

Figure 17
Assessing Concepts of Books and Comprehension of Text

Student Name: _____ Date: _____

	YES	NO
Concepts of Books		
Knows a book is for reading		
Can identify the front, back, top, and bottom of a book		
Can turn the pages properly		
Knows the difference between the print and the pictures		
Knows pictures are related to what the print says on a page		
Knows where to begin reading		
Knows what a title is		
Knows what an author is		
Knows what an illustrator is		
Comprehension of Text		
"Reads" storybooks resulting in well-formed stories		
Participates in story reading by narrating as the teacher reads		
Retells stories		
Includes story structure elements in story retellings		
Setting		
Theme		
Plot episodes		
Resolution		
Recognizes expository text features and structures		
Table of contents		
Headings		
Diagrams		

(continued)

Figure 17 *(continued)*	YES	NO
Recognizes expository text structures		
Description		
Compare and contrast		
Cause and effect		
Problem and solution		
Exemplification		
Responds to text after listening with literal comments or questions		
Responds to text after listening with interpretive comments or questions		
Participates and responds during		
Partner reading		
Buddy reading		
Mental imagery		
Think-alouds		
Participates in fluency activities		
Echo chanting		
Choral chanting		
Audio recording–assisted listening		

Comments:

CHAPTER 4

Using Children's Literature Throughout the Preschool Curriculum

Many preschool classrooms follow an integrated school day, in which skills from all content areas are taught within the context of a topic of study. In this interdisciplinary approach, study topics come from children's interests and experiences. Learning experiences are socially interactive and process oriented, giving children time to explore and experiment with varied materials. If, for example, a class is studying dinosaurs, the children talk, read, and write about dinosaurs; do art projects related to dinosaurs; and sing dinosaur-related songs. In doing so, they learn about dinosaurs and develop skills in other content areas, such as science, social studies, and math. Children's literature and literacy activities play an important role in this integrated school day and provide a rich resource of information, ideas, and experiences (Pappas, Kiefer, & Levstik, 1995).

Preschool children should be involved in literature activities on a daily basis. Literature activities need to be modeled to encourage children's interest. Table 6 provides a list of suggested activities.

> Preschool children should be involved in literature activities on a daily basis. Literature activities need to be modeled to encourage children's interest.

Literature, Literacy, and Play in Preschool Themes

Literacy development relies on active collaboration with adults and peers; it builds on what the child already knows, and thrives on the support and guidance of others. Play provides these elements in meaningful and functional contexts. Play is essential for social, emotional, physical, and intellectual development; it enhances children's language and a number of activities in which children participate (Morrow, 1990; Neuman & Roskos, 1990). As children play, they incorporate functional uses of literacy into their play themes. Children collaborate with their peers as they engage in attempted and conventional reading and writing.

Table 6
Literature Activities for the Preschool Classroom

Frequency	Activities
Daily	1. Read or tell narrative and expository stories to children. 2. Encourage student participation in storybook reading. 3. Discuss books. Discussion topics should include both literal aspects, such as story sequence and details, and interpretive aspects, such as opinions and feelings. 4. Relate discussions to the child's life experiences. 5. Allow children to check out books from the classroom library. 6. Highlight interesting words found in books. 7. Have children keep the library corner neat and organized.
Weekly	1. Have an assortment of adults (principal or director, custodian, school nurse, secretary, parents and grandparents) read to the class. 2. Discuss authors and illustrators. 3. Write to authors. 4. Have older children read to younger children. 5. Have children read in pairs. 6. Play audio recordings and video adaptations of storybooks. 7. Use literature across the curriculum in content area lessons. 8. Use art to respond to books (e.g., draw a mural of a story, use art techniques modeled after a particular illustrator). 9. Tell stories using a creative storytelling technique. 10. Have children tell stories with and without props. 11. Have children act out stories. 12. Prepare recipes related to stories (e.g., make spaghetti after reading *Strega Nona: An Old Tale* by Tomie dePaola). 13. Read stories that were shown on television. 14. Make class books and individual books; bind them and store in the library corner. 15. Sing songs and read related storybooks (e.g., *I Know an Old Lady Who Swallowed a Fly* by Nadine Bernard Westcott). 16. Make bulletin boards related to books. 17. Discuss proper ways to care for and handle books. 18. Read, recite, and write poetry. 19. Provide time for children to select their own books to look at independently a few times a week. 20. Reread favorite storybooks.
Monthly	1. Circulate 20 new books into the library corner every month. 2. Introduce new books added to the library corner. 3. Feature new books on the open-faced bookshelves.

(continued)

Table 6 *(continued)*	
A Few Times a Year, if Possible	1. Give bookmarks to children.
	2. Give each child a book as a gift.
	3. Have a book celebration day (e.g., dress up as book characters, tell stories to each other, show videos).

It is important to embed literature and literacy activities within the play curriculum. When enriched to promote literacy learning, the dramatic play area is filled with theme-related materials to enhance and extend the current unit of study. Materials for reading and writing are provided to support the play theme; as they play, children read, write, speak, and listen to one another, using literacy in functional ways.

It is difficult to isolate the use of children's literature from play activities. Therefore, we will discuss literacy and play in general terms, with a special emphasis on children's literature. The following example from a preschool classroom shows the collaborative and interactive nature of literacy development (see Figure 18 for a photo of the classroom veterinary clinic discussed in this vignette).

• • • • • • • • • • • • • •

Ms. Casey has designed a veterinary clinic dramatic play center in her preschool classroom to enrich a unit of study on pets. The classroom veterinary clinic includes a waiting room; chairs; a table filled with magazines, children's literature, and pamphlets about pet care; posters about pets; office hour notices; a "No Smoking" sign; and a sign advising visitors to "Check in with the nurse when arriving." A nurse's desk holds patient forms on clipboards, a telephone, an address and telephone book, appointment cards, a calendar, and a computer for recording appointments and patient records. The examination area features patient folders, prescription pads, white coats, masks, gloves, cotton swabs, a toy doctor's kit, and stuffed animals to serve as patients.

Ms. Casey guides children in the use of the various materials in the clinic by reminding the children to read in waiting areas, fill out forms with prescriptions or appointment times, and fill out forms with information about an animal's condition and treatment. In addition to

Figure 18
Classroom Veterinary Clinic

giving directions, Ms. Casey models behaviors by playing with the children whenever new materials are introduced in the play center. For example, while waiting for the doctor to see her stuffed-animal patient, Ms. Casey reads a picture storybook to her puppy, and then reads a magazine herself.

Several children's literacy behaviors were observed in this setting. For example, Jessica waits to see the doctor. She tells her stuffed toy dog, Sam, not to worry, that the doctor won't hurt him. She asks Jenny, who is waiting with her stuffed toy cat, Muffin, what the kitten's problem is. The girls agonize over the ailments of their pets. After a while they stop talking and Jessica picks up a book from the table and pretends to read *How Do Dinosaurs Eat Their Food?* (Yolen & Teague, 2005) to Sam. Jessica shows Sam the pictures as she reads.

Jennie runs into the doctor's office shouting, "My dog got runned over by a car!" The doctor bandages the dog's leg; the two children then decide that the incident must be reported to the police.

Before calling the police, they get out the telephone book and turn to a map to find the spot where the dog had been hit. Then, they call the police on the toy phone to report the incident.

Jonah examines Preston's teddy bear and writes a report in the patient's folder. He reads his scribble writing out loud and says, "This teddy bear's blood pressure is 29 points. He should take 62 pills an hour until he is better and keep warm and go to bed." While he reads, he shows Preston what he wrote so he understands what to do. He asks his nurse to type the notes into the computer.

● ● ● ● ● ● ● ● ● ● ● ● ● ●

In this vignette, we see a play setting that provides children with print to read, and with materials that encourage writing. Children play together and engage in literacy behaviors as they play.

Literacy-Enriched Play Settings

Designing a dramatic play area to match a topic of study makes the content more meaningful for children. Modify the dramatic play center whenever you begin to study a new theme. Be sure to guide and model the use of materials. It can be useful to record literacy behaviors in the play area (Neuman & Roskos, 1993). This will provide information about what children are doing and which play settings stimulate literacy behavior. Assessment of literacy behavior in play settings should be done by the teacher about once a month.

Almost any topic of study can be enhanced with a literacy-enriched play setting. The following are play settings, with suggestions for literacy materials that relate to the theme.

Post Office. Include shoeboxes, stickers for stamps, envelopes, paper and pencils, baskets to sort different types of mail, a map to show where mail travels, as well as resource books on related topics.

The Zoo. Provide plastic or stuffed animals, magazines and books about animals, blocks to build cages for the animals, buttons or foam shapes as food for the animals.

Doctor's Office. Include a telephone, desk, clip boards, paper and pencils, dolls, bandages, posters of the human body, books about nutrition and health, pillows and a bed, and white jackets for doctors.

Supermarket.   Supply pretend food, empty cereal and pasta boxes, empty milk cartons, shopping baskets, paper or plastic shopping bags, cash registers, and pretend money. Children can take turns being shoppers and check-out clerks. Give children a list of groceries to buy to encourage word recognition.

Literature, Literacy, and Art in Preschool Themes

Art experiences allow children to explore and experiment with interesting materials such as finger paints and watercolors; colored pencils, felt-tip markers, and crayons; construction paper, tissue paper, foil, and transparent wrap; paste, scissors, clay, and play dough. To link art and literacy within a theme, teachers can instruct children to create theme-related pictures. For example, after reading the book *Autumn* (Saunders-Smith, 1998), the class can discuss fruits and colors of fall and then make pictures using colors such as yellow, orange, green, brown, and red. Some children will make representational drawings; others will do scribble drawings. All are acceptable. The pictures can be fastened together to make a fall book.

Discussing children's book illustrators and illustration styles is a natural way of linking art and literature for young children. For example, Betsy Lewin, illustrator of *Giggle, Giggle, Quack* and *Click, Clack, Moo, Cows That Type* (2000), used a variety of different brushes to illustrate characters and emotions. Leo Lionni, author and illustrator of *Frederick* (1991), created some of his artwork using crayons. Eric Carle, author and illustrator of *The Very Hungry Caterpillar* (1994) and *The Very Busy Spider* (1989), writes mostly about animals and insects. He uses bright colors and his art has a distinctive, bold style.

Young children can learn to distinguish some of the techniques of well-known illustrators and talk about how they are similar or different. They can select materials used by these illustrators for their own pictures.

Literature, Literacy, and Music in Preschool Themes

Music provides abundant opportunities for literacy development. Songs introduce children to new words and word patterns, expanding their vocabularies and building their **phonological awareness**. When songs are written on charts and teachers point to the words to track the print across the page, children learn important print concepts.

Songs based on current topics of study are an essential element of the preschool curriculum, and books based on songs are a great addition to any classroom library. When studying farms, for example, select books to feature such as *Old McDonald Had a Farm* (Cabrera, 2008) and *Go Tell Aunt Rhody* (Quackenbush, 1973). You can read the words and sing the songs with children. Many holiday songs have been adapted into books: *Over the River and Through the Wood* (Child, 1999) and *Five Little Pumpkins* (Van Rynbach, 2004) are two popular examples. Listening to music inspires children to form mental images about a theme. For this reason, music is a rich source for generating descriptive language. Ask children to close their eyes while listening to the music and think about the theme they are studying. Ask them to describe images that come to mind.

Literature, Literacy, Science, and Social Studies in Preschool Themes

Science and social studies are probably the two content areas that provide the greatest opportunities for literacy development because topics in these subject areas typically generate enthusiasm and a purpose for reading and writing. For instance, a unit about the farm can promote oral language development through discussions about farm work, different types of farms, and farm animals. Children can generate word lists of farm animals, crops, and jobs. Pictures of farm scenes, a trip to a farm, or a visit by a farmer generate discussion, reading, and writing. By reading picture books about farms to the class, teachers can encourage positive attitudes toward books, enhance children's vocabulary, and share information about farming. *The Milk Makers* (Gibbons, 1987), *Barn Dance!* (Hutchins, 2007), and *My Trip to the Farm* (Mayer, 2002) are just a few children's classics that deal with rural life. *Big Red Barn* (Brown, 1989) features rhymed text and illustrations introducing the different animals that live on a farm. Children will enjoy picking up the books on their own, sharing them with friends, and retelling and role-playing the stories. A farm visit can be retold in stories or drawings and then be bound into class books.

Science experiments and food preparation offer other opportunities for discussion and vocabulary enrichment. Whether the topic is the weather or plants, collections of books that are both informational *and* narrative can

> Science and social studies are probably the two content areas that provide the greatest opportunities for literacy development because topics in these subject areas typically generate enthusiasm and a purpose for reading and writing.

Figure 19
Reading a Big Book About Spiderwebs

be provided to enhance the child's knowledge. Figure 19 shows two children reading a Big Book about spiderwebs during a **thematic unit** on spiders.

Literature, Literacy, and Math in Preschool Themes

Math and literacy are not incompatible. Math-related storybooks introduce young children to numeracy concepts and extend their math vocabulary. The following are just a few of the excellent math storybooks available for the preschool classroom:

- Bang, M. (1991). *Ten, nine, eight*. New York: HarperCollins.
- Ehlert, L. (1992). *Fish eyes*. San Diego, CA: Harcourt.
- Grossman, B. (1998). *My little sister ate one hare*. New York: Random House.
- Roth, C. (2002). *Ten dirty pigs, ten clean pigs*. New York: North-South.

Children ask for the skills they need to understand content information because they have an interest in it (Manning, Manning, & Long, 1994; Walmsley, 1994). For example, during a discussion of a transportation theme in Suzanne's kindergarten class, children asked for even more materials than she had already made available in the several centers. Books on transportation led to requests for books on space travel and various maps of places. The interesting experiences provided for the children made them eager to learn more.

Conducting a Thematic Unit

Theme topics can be selected by the teacher and the children. Giving students choices concerning what they will learn is important. When a topic is selected, invite the children to brainstorm what they would like to know about (Rand, 1994). To gain a better understanding of the role of literature in a thematic unit, consider the following example from a preschool unit on "Animals Around the World." Although the unit includes activities for all content areas, here we will examine only the activities that involve children's literature.

Preparing for the Unit

To begin the theme on animals around the world, prepare the room so that the theme is evident to those who enter your classroom. Add new, theme-related materials to all classroom areas, including the literacy center. For example, in the **writing center**, you can include animal-shaped blank books and a message board on which to share the morning message. In the library corner, you can include storybooks and informational texts on animals as well as pamphlets and magazines about animal habitat. Table 7 lists several animal-related picture books; additional suggestions can be found in Appendix A.

Activities for the Theme

The following activities are initiated through the use of children's literature. Each relates to the theme "Animals Around the World."

Literacy

Objective: Create an alphabet book that reviews many animal words learned in the unit.

Table 7
Animals Around the World: Suggested Picture Books for the Library Corner

Aliki. (1999). *My visit to the zoo*. New York: HarperCollins.

Andreae, G., & Parker-Rees, G. (2001). *Giraffes can't dance*. London, England: Orchard.

Bancroft, H. (1997). *Animals in winter*. New York: HarperCollins.

Beall, P.C., & Nipp, S.H. (2006). *Wee sing, animals, animals, animals*. New York: Price Stern Sloan.

Campbell, R. (2007). *Dear zoo: A lift-the-flap book*. New York: Simon & Schuster.

Carle, E. (1998). *1, 2, 3 to the zoo: A counting book*. New York: Putnam.

Chanko, P. (1998). *Baby animals learn*. New York: Scholastic.

Chessen, B., & Chanko, P. (1998). *Animal homes*. New York: Scholastic.

Jenkins, S. (2006). *Almost gone: The world's rarest animals* (Lets-Read-and-Find-Out series). New York: HarperCollins.

Keats, E.J. (1974). *Pet show*. New York: Aladdin.

Lauber, P., & Keller, H. (1995). *Who eats what? Food chains and food webs*. New York: HarperCollins.

Mora, P., & Cushman, D. (2006). *Marimba! Animales from A to Z*. New York: Houghton Mifflin.

Rabe, T. (2007). *My, oh my—A butterfly! All about butterflies* (Cat in the Hat's Learning Library). New York: Random House.

Relf, P., & Stevenson, N. (1995). *The Magic School Bus hops home: A book about animal habitats*. New York: Scholastic.

Satoh, A., & Toda, K. (1996). *Animal faces*. La Jolla, CA: Kane/Miller.

Staff of National Geographic, McKay, G., & McGhe, K. (2006). *National Geographic encyclopedia of animals*. Washington, DC: National Geographic Society.

Steig, W., & Puncel, M. (trans.). (1997). *Doctor de soto* (Spanish Ed.). New York: Farrar, Straus and Giroux.

Taylor, B. (1998). *A day at the farm*. New York: DK Publishing.

Wallace, K. (2003). *Trip to the zoo* (DK Readers series). New York: DK Publishing.

Procedure: An "Amazing Animal Alphabet Book" will be made and photocopied for each child in the class. Each letter will represent a different animal (e.g., *A*—armadillo, *B*—bird, *C*—chimpanzee, *D*—dog, *E*—elephant, *F*—fish, etc.). The students will read the letters and words with the teacher and each other.

Art

Objective: Participate in a creative art activity related to a storybook that includes learning about animal faces.

Procedure: After reading the book *Animal Faces* (Satoh & Toda, 1996), discuss the similarities and differences among various animal faces. Provide students with materials such as paper plates, crayons, construction paper, macaroni, and feathers to make their own zoo face masks. A piece of string can be tied to either side to fit the mask around their heads.

Music

Objective: Identify vocabulary for animal names by singing theme-related songs.

Procedure: A collection of animal songs can be found in *Wee Sing, Animals, Animals, Animals* (Beall & Nipp, 2006). Sing the songs found in the book. On a large piece of paper list the animals mentioned and have the children copy the words in a writing journal.

Science

Objective: Discuss the metamorphosis of a caterpillar into a butterfly. Read the story and have students draw pictures and write words to demonstrate comprehension.

Procedure: Read the book *My, Oh My—A Butterfly! All About Butterflies* (Rabe, 2007) to learn about the metamorphosis of a caterpillar. Students can draw pictures and add corresponding vocabulary words to illustrate the miraculous transformation.

Social Studies

Objective: Match the animals with their country of origin. Become more familiar with world geography.

Procedure: Have children color pictures of adult and baby animals and paste on construction paper. Display a map of the world for students to paste the animal in the appropriate region. The book *Animal Homes* (Chessen & Chanko, 1998) will help students develop content knowledge.

Math

Objective: Use math vocabulary when retelling a story. Match numbers and objects.

Procedure: Read a story related to animals such as *1, 2, 3 to the Zoo: A Counting Book* (Carle, 1998). Ask the class to retell the story using props for the animals that are in the book. Have children count the different types of animals on each page of the book and match the numeral to the corresponding animal.

Use Table 6 to see how many of the activities you use on a daily basis, weekly basis, and monthly basis using literature. Figure out where you can improve.

With your colleagues, select a professional development book about the use of children's literature in preschool, which could be this book or another. Come to meetings having read a chapter and putting the ideas into practice. Discuss and reflect upon the chapter and how things went in your classroom.

Share general ideas you like that you do with literature with your peers so you can learn from each other.

Check your plans and your centers in art, music, play, social studies, and science to be sure you are including books appropriate for what is going on in those centers. Add titles to suit the center or theme being used at the time.

Write a thematic unit and be sure to include literature and literacy in the content areas such as play, music, art, social studies, and science.

CHAPTER 5

Reading With Children at Home

• • • • • • • • • • • • •

Mrs. Jones spreads the newspaper on the table as her 5-year-old grandson sits next to her. She takes out the sports section since they had just seen a college football game that was written about in the local paper.

Darren:	What was the score again? I forget.
Mrs. Jones:	Let's look together and figure it out. Can you read those numbers?
Darren:	That's Rutgers, 13, and Syracuse, 7.
Mrs. Jones:	Very good.
Darren:	Who is that player in the picture?
Mrs. Jones:	[She gets out the book they bought at the game and looks to see who #23 was. When they find out, Mrs. Jones reads about him to Darren.]
Darren:	How far is Syracuse? Can we go there?
Mrs. Jones:	It is about a four-hour drive to get there. [She gets out a map and shows Darren where he lives in New Jersey and where Syracuse is in New York.]

• • • • • • • • • • • •

In the preceding vignette—a conversation between a boy and his grandmother—the discussion made use of new vocabulary, reading, math, and geography. The newspaper was the form of literature that served as the basis of the discussion.

As illustrated in this vignette, children's first and most enduring teachers are the family members who care for them. The success of any preschool literacy program largely depends on the literacy environment at home. Schools must involve parents as

> Children's first and most enduring teachers are the family members who care for them. The success of any preschool literacy program largely depends on the literacy environment at home. Schools must involve parents as an integral part of their literacy programs.

an integral part of their literacy programs. Because families come in many forms, we use the term *parent* to refer to any adult who is responsible for the child's care at home.

Family Literacy: Why Is It Important?

I (Lesley) can attest to the vital role of the home in the development of early literacy. From the day my grandchild James was born, he has been read to by his mother, his father, and all four of his grandparents. Every day, he has snuggled up for storytime, always in the same chair, sitting in the reader's lap. By 5 months, sweet baby James would listen as he was read to. My daughter chose mostly board books with short stories and only a few words on each page, such as *The Very Hungry Caterpillar* (Carle, 1994). As he was read to, James focused intently on the brightly colored pictures. First he would look serious; next he would smile broadly. He frequently reached out to touch the books. Occasionally he made cooing sounds that seemed like attempts to imitate the reading voice. Through this daily experience, he became familiar with storybook readings and welcomed them.

As months went by, James responded to books in new ways. By 10 months, he could turn the pages of the book. By 12 months, he pointed to pictures and made sounds as if naming objects or characters. The family responded with pleasure; this attention and encouragement motivated James to keep exploring books. We talked about the words and pictures, expanding story concepts. Storybook reading was a pleasant and relaxing ritual that everyone looked forward to.

By the time he was 15 months old, James could be found sitting on the floor "reading" a book. He knew how to hold the book right side up, he knew which was the beginning of the book and which was the end, and he knew how to turn the pages. He looked at the pictures and chanted in tones similar to the sound of the reading. His language was not understandable, but from a distance one might think that he was reading. Actually he was—not in the conventional manner, but by demonstrating early literacy behavior.

James had an accessible shelf of books in his room. My daughter kept a crate of books with his toys on the floor of a closet, and he was free to use them at all times. James saw his parents reading, and at times he joined them with his own books. His knowledge about books and reading did not just happen. Rather, it developed within an environment that fostered literacy through the guidance, modeling, and encouragement of supportive adults.

Promoting Literacy Development in the Home

Children's family members frequently ask teachers what they can do at home to help their children learn to read and write. When families provide a rich literacy environment at home, teaching reading and writing becomes easier for both the teacher and the child at school. Schools need to take responsibility for sharing information in the community about activities that families can implement at home before their children enter preschool. For example, family workshops can be held for parents of children who are not yet of school age, and schools can distribute booklets about literacy development at home from birth to age 3.

> When families provide a rich literacy environment at home, teaching reading and writing becomes easier for both the teacher and the child at school. Schools need to take responsibility for sharing information in the community about activities that families can implement at home before their children enter preschool.

The following factors affect the quality of the literacy environment in the home (Leichter, 1984):

- Interpersonal interactions—the literacy experiences shared by children, parents, siblings, and other individuals in the home
- Physical environment—literacy materials in the home
- Emotional and motivational climate—family attitudes and aspirations for literacy achievement

This means that books, magazines, and newspapers are read and are discussed among family members. Children have access to many types of reading and writing materials and are encouraged to use them in their daily lives. Parents let children know that they value reading and writing.

In the following sections, we will suggest materials and strategies for reading with children at home that preschool teachers can share with families. Because early exposure to print is critical for successful literacy development, we will discuss reading with children from birth onward. Parents must be made aware of the work they need to do at home with books before children enter preschool.

Materials to Read in the Home

Children's books should be made available throughout the home—in the kitchen, the bathroom, and the playroom. Setting up a library corner in each child's bedroom provides children with easy access to books and helps make reading an integral part of a family's daily routine. If a bookshelf is not available, books can be stored in a cardboard box or plastic crate. Before babies are crawling or walking, books can be brought to them in cribs and playpens; waterproof books are perfect for bathtubs.

A well-stocked home library contains many types of books. A more complete list of appropriate books for young children can be found in Appendix A. For babies up to 18 months, brightly colored concept books with cardboard, plastic, or cloth pages are ideal. They must be safe, with rounded edges, and sturdy enough to withstand chewing and other rough treatment. As the child enters the preschool years and beyond, nursery rhymes, fairy tales, folktales, realistic literature, informational books, picture books, alphabet books, number books, poetry, books related to favorite television programs, and easy-to-read books (i.e., those with limited vocabularies, large print, and pictures closely associated with the text) should be made available. Children's magazines also offer attractive print material and are a special treat if they come in the mail. In addition to children's literature, print material for adults, including books, magazines, newspapers, and work-related material, should be obvious in the home (Applebee, Langer, & Mullis, 1988; Hannon, 1995).

Reading as a Home Activity

Children who are read to regularly by parents, siblings, or other individuals in the home and who have family members who read recreationally become early readers and show a natural interest in books (Bus, van IJzendoorn, & Pellegrini, 1995; Sulzby & Teale, 1987). This is not surprising. Through frequent storybook readings, children become familiar with book language and realize the function of written language. Storybook readings are almost always pleasurable, which builds a desire for and interest in reading (Cullinan, 1987; Huck, 1992).

Teachers should encourage family members to read to their children daily. Reading can begin the day a child is born, although an infant's ability to listen attentively is generally limited and varies from one reading to the next. An infant may prefer to chew on the book or pound it rather than listen to it. However, babies read to from birth begin to be attentive in storybook reading situations sooner than those who are not read to (Morrow, 2005).

Reading to Children at Home From Birth to Age 8

When babies are read to often, they become responsive to books. From birth to 3 months, a child's attention to book reading is erratic. The baby who stares at the pictures and seems content and quiet can be considered receptive. If the baby wiggles, shows discomfort, or cries, the adult should stop reading and try another time.

From 3 to 6 months, babies become more obviously involved in book readings. They begin to focus on pictures and to listen. Often, they will grab for a book, pound it, and try to put it in their mouths. As long as they seem content, they are involved with the reading.

Six- to nine-month-olds can be purposefully involved in storybook readings. They might try to turn pages, respond to changes in the reader's intonation, or make sounds and movements to demonstrate involvement and pleasure. They sometimes begin to show preferences for books that have been read to them before.

One-year-olds will take a leadership role in turning pages, and they often babble along with the reader in tones that sound like reading. They show strong involvement in being read to; when they see a familiar book, they look for things that they remember from earlier readings such as a brightly colored page.

By 15 months, babies who have been read to can tell which is the front and which is the back of a book, and if the book is right-side up. They begin to identify and name characters in the book. They "read" along with the adult, verbalizing a great deal (Burns, Griffin, & Snow, 1999).

Parents should make reading a ritual; it should be done at the same time and in the same place each day. Bedtime is many children's favorite time to listen to stories and bedtime stories are a good reading habit to establish. Both children and older family members look forward to sharing a book at the end of the day. Reading to children before they go to sleep has a calming effect; it helps establish a routine for children, who can eventually read by themselves before going to bed.

Reading to children should not end when they begin to read themselves. When children are able to read, the bedtime-story tradition can evolve into the child's reading to another family member, or it can continue with adults reading aloud books above the reading level of the child. Four- to seven-year-olds are often interested in books with chapters, but are not yet ready to read them on their own. Family members can take this opportunity to motivate young readers by reading aloud more challenging pieces of literature.

Another important way of motivating young readers is to make sure they always have access to new reading material that is of interest to them. Parents should keep track of what their child has read. Adults need to continually put new books in children's hands, even as children grow older and seem to have established the reading habit. Supporting children's reading habits helps children maintain interest in reading.

In addition to reading to their children and reading themselves, families can make a point of providing time for the family to read together. Sitting together around the kitchen table or in the living room, with each family member reading his or her own book, is an enriching activity for all. Talking about what family members are reading is an important experience as well.

Strategies for Reading at Home

Verbal interaction between a family member and child during storybook readings has a major influence on literacy development (Cochran-Smith, 1984; Ninio, 1980). When parents interact with their children during storybook reading, they define words, repeat information, and explain ideas, enhancing children's literacy development (Heath, 1982; Morrow, 1987). Children begin to respond to storybook readings with questions and comments, which become more complex over time as children demonstrate more sophisticated thinking about printed material. Research on home storybook readings has identified a number of interactive behaviors that affect the quality of read-aloud activities. Those behaviors include questioning, scaffolding (modeling dialogue and responses), praising, offering information, directing discussion, sharing personal reactions, and relating concepts to life experiences (Edwards, 1995; Roser & Martinez, 1985; Taylor & Strickland, 1986). Figure 20 shows a father directing discussion during a storybook reading, which enhances the child's involvement.

The following discussion (Morrow, 1986) between a mother and her 4-year-old son, Ian, took place at the beginning of a storybook reading and illustrates how an adult can invite and scaffold responses. As a result of his mother's prompts, responses, and support, Ian pursues his questions and receives additional information.

Figure 20
Father–Son Storybook Reading

• • • • • • • • • • • • • • •

Mother: Are you ready for our story today, Natalie? This is a new book. I've never read it to you before. It's about a spider that is very busy spinning her web.

Natalie: Hey, what does that say? [points to the title on the front cover]

Mother: That's called a title. It says *The Very Busy Spider*. That's the name of the book. See, it's right here, too: *The Very Busy Spider*.

Natalie: [long pause, then points to the words] *The Very Busy Spider*?

Mother:	Right, you read it. See, you know how to read.
Natalie:	It says, *The Very Busy Spider*? [points again with finger]
Mother:	You read it again. Wow, you really know how to read!
Natalie:	Um, now read the book and I'll read it, too.

Natalie's mother reads the story. Each time they come to the text "The spider didn't answer. She was very busy spinning her web," she pauses and looks at Natalie, points to the words, and exaggerates her reading of the sentence. After two such episodes, Natalie no longer needs prompting and points and reads along.

• • • • • • • • • • • • • •

Family Involvement in Your Literacy Program: General Guidelines About What Teachers Can Do

Teachers need to view parents as partners in the development of literacy. Every teacher has the responsibility to inform families on a regular basis about what is happening in school and how they can help their child. Teachers need to involve family members in school activities during the day and provide activities for family members to do at home. Family members need to feel that they are welcome in school; they need opportunities to offer input about what they would like their child to learn, to express how they feel about what happens in school, and to offer suggestions for change. Table 8 offers suggestions for parent–teacher partnership, and Figure 21 provides a form that parents can use during parent–teacher conferences to contribute information about their child's progress.

Long before children enter preschool, teachers need to communicate to families about the necessity for rich literacy environments. Information can be disseminated at a special meeting for expectant parents, in hospital maternity wards, in obstetrician's and pediatrician's offices, in churches, synagogues, and community agencies. A succinct handout such as Promoting Early Literacy at Home (see Figure 22) will be a helpful start and can be printed in different languages found in your community.

Table 8
Tips for Promoting Parent Involvement in the Preschool Literacy Program

1. **Communicate goals.** At the beginning of the school year, send home the goals to be achieved in literacy development for the age group you teach in an easy-to-understand format.

2. **Publish a newsletter.** With each new unit of instruction or concept being taught in literacy, send a newsletter to let family members know what you are studying and what they can do to help. Include titles of books they can get from the library to read at home.

3. **Meet with parents.** Invite parents to school programs, parent–teacher conferences, and public meetings about curriculum decisions. Sponsor informational workshops on topics such as reading with children and selecting books to share at home.

4. **Encourage families to assist in the classroom.** Invite parents and grandparents to help with literacy activities such as bookbinding, reading with children, taking written dictation of children's stories, and supervising independent activities while teachers work with small groups and individual children. Whenever parents visit the classroom, encourage them to work with their children. For instance, if parents visit during center time, they can read and write with their children, see what the literacy environment is like at school, and become a more integral part of the child's literacy development.

5. **Send home activities and encourage feedback.** Extend the work you do in the classroom with take-home activities such as reading books aloud, visiting the library, using cookbooks, writing notes, writing in journals together, and watching and talking about programs on television. Whenever you send home activities for parents and children to do together, ask families to provide written feedback about the experience. Such feedback provides insight into what happens at home, holds families accountable for participating, and helps you plan future activities.

6. **Celebrate the families in your classroom.** Invite parents and grandparents to school to share special skills they have, to talk about their cultural heritage, and so forth.

7. **Send home notes when a child is doing well.** Don't wait to send notes just when problems arise.

8. **Provide lists of literature for family members to share with their children.** (Appendix A suggests books on a variety of topics.)

9. **Include family members in helping to assess their child's progress.** Provide forms for family members to fill out about their child's literacy activities and things they do with their child at home. Have them contribute information about their child's progress at parent conferences.

Figure 21
Child Progress Information Form

Checklist: Observing My Child's Literary Growth

Child's Name: _____ Date: _____

	Always	Sometimes	Never	Comments
1. My child asks to be read to.				
2. My child will read or look at a book alone.				
3. My child understands what is read to him/her, or what he/she reads to himself/herself.				
4. My child handles a book properly, knows how to turn pages, and knows that print is read from left to right.				
5. My child will pretend to read or read to me.				
6. My child participates in the reading of a story, with rhymes and repeated phrases.				
7. My child will write with me.				
8. My child will write alone.				
9. My child will talk about what he or she has written.				
10. My child reads print in the environment, such as sign and labels.				
11. My child likes school.				

Comments about your child:

Note. From Lesley Mandel Morrow, *Literacy Development in the Early Years: Helping Children Read and Write,* Fifth Edition. Published by Allyn & Bacon, Boston, MA. Copyright © 2005 by Pearson Education. Reprinted by permission of the publisher.

Figure 22
Promoting Early Literacy at Home

Your child's ability to read and write depends a lot on the things you do at home from the time he or she is born. The following list suggests materials, activities, and attitudes that are important in helping your child learn to read and write. Check off the things you already do. Then, try to do something on the list that you have not done before.

Materials

__ Have a space at home for books and magazines for your child.

__ If you can, subscribe to a magazine for your child.

__ Keep reading materials on hand for everyone in your home. Visit the library and fill your home with books, magazines, and newspapers for children and adults.

__ Provide materials that will encourage children to tell or create their own stories, such as puppets, dolls, and audiobooks.

__ Provide materials for writing, such as crayons, markers, pencils, and paper in different sizes.

Activities

__ Read or look at books, magazines, or the newspaper with your child. Talk about what you look at or read.

__ Tell stories together about books, about your family, and about things that you do.

__ Look at and talk about written material you have such as catalogues, advertisements, work-related materials, and mail.

__ Provide a model for your child by reading and writing at times when your child can see you.

__ Write with your child and talk about what you write.

__ Point out print in your home, such as words on food boxes or recipes, directions on medicine, or instructions on things that require assembly.

__ Point out print in the neighborhood, such as road signs and names of stores.

__ Visit the post office, supermarket, or zoo and get books to read about these places. On the way home, talk about what you saw. When you get home, draw and write about the experience.

__ Use print to communicate with your child. Leave notes for each other. Make to-do lists, grocery lists, and lists for holiday shopping.

Foster Positive Attitudes Toward Reading and Writing

__ Reward your child's attempts at reading and writing, even if they are not perfect, by offering praise. Say kind words like, "What nice work you do," "I'm happy to see you are reading," and "I'm happy to see you are writing. Can I help you?"

__ Answer your child's questions about reading and writing.

__ Be sure that reading and writing are enjoyable experiences.

__ Display your child's work in your home.

__ Visit school when your child asks. Volunteer to help at school, attend programs in which your child is participating, and attend meetings and family conferences. This lets your child know you care about him or her and school.

What Makes a Family Involvement Literacy Program Successful?

Because no two communities are the same, family literacy programs need to be tailored to the needs of the individuals they serve. Table 9 offers some tested tips for program success.

Table 10 offers a list of resources for teachers to share with families. The picture books listed are representative of diverse cultural backgrounds. Each book illustrates a special relationship between family and extended family members.

Family members are children's first and most enduring teachers. Quality preschools engage families as an integral part of language and literacy programs—both in school and at home. Reach out to parents and make them an integral part of your reading program.

PROFESSIONAL DEVELOPMENT FOR PRE- AND INSERVICE TEACHERS

Make a strong effort to include parents in your program. Have parents come to school for an information session and model good storybook reading for them, identify good characteristics of children's literature, and make suggestions of good children's literature to read to their children. Help them to understand the importance of exposure to many genres. Model storytelling with and without props for parents. Have parents make a story prop to bring home. Have parents complete the form in Figure 21 so you have some insight as to what parents are doing with children at home and what your children are doing with literature at home.

Let your parents know about themes being studied and invite them to read a book about the theme. If they have books from other countries, they are welcome to read them in their own language if they wish. The teacher can read it first in English.

Check Table 8 and see how many of the activities suggested you do. Try new ones and reflect with your peers how they worked out.

Create a plan for your own professional development that deals with enhancing your knowledge about using children's literature and developing comprehension skills in preschool.

Table 9
Tips for Family Literacy Programs

- Respect and understand the diversity of the families you serve.
- Be aware of the different languages used in children's homes within the community. Translate materials so that everyone can understand them.
- Accommodate all schedules by holding meetings at varied times of the day and days of the week.
- Provide transportation if family members do not have a way of getting to meetings.
- Provide child care at meetings.
- Serve food and refreshments.
- At family meetings, offer ideas and materials that families can share at home.
- Encourage family members' participation in school activities during school hours.

Table 10
Family Resources

Resource Type	Resource
Children's Books About Families	Bunting, E. (2004). *Can you do this, Old Badger?* San Diego, CA: Harcourt. Darian, S. (1996). *Grandpa's garden*. Nevada City, CA: Dawn Publications. Downey, R. (2001). *Love is a family*. New York: HarperCollins. Fox, M. (1997). *Sophie*. San Diego, CA: Harcourt. Guback, G. (1994). *Luka's quilt*. New York: Greenwillow. Hausherr, R. (1997). *Celebrating families*. New York: Scholastic. Katz, K. (2007). *Daddy hugs*. New York: Simon & Schuster. McCormick, W. (2002). *Daddy, will you miss me?* New York: Aladdin. Parr, T. (2003). *The family book*. Boston: Little, Brown. Reid, M. (1995). The *button box*. New York: Penguin. Tsubakiyama, M.H. (1999). *Mei-Mei loves the morning*. Morton Grove, IL: Albert Whitman. Wild, M. (1995). *Remember me*. Morton Grove, IL: Albert Whitman. Winch, J. (2000). *Keeping up with grandma*. New York: Holiday House.
Additional Family Literacy Resources for Parents and Educators	International Reading Association. (1997). *Explore the playground of books: Tips for parents of beginning readers* [Brochure]. Newark, DE: Author. International Reading Association. (1997). *Get ready to read! Tips for parents of young children* [Brochure]. Newark, DE: Author. International Reading Association. (1999). *Beginning literacy and your child: A guide to helping your baby or preschooler become a reader* [Booklet]. Newark, DE: Author. National Association for the Education of Young Children. (2004). *Raising a reader, raising a writer: How parents can help* [Brochure]. Washington, DC: Author. Lipson, E.R. (2000). New York Times *parent's guide to the best books for children*. New York: Crown. Trelease, J. (1985). *The read-aloud handbook*. New York: Penguin.

This book demonstrates the value of using children's literature in preschool and offers teachers practical methods of helping young children enjoy literature and draw information from books. First, we discussed children's literature and its effect on social, emotional, and intellectual development. Next, we examined different genres of literature and described how to integrate children's literature into content area subjects such as dramatic play, art, music, science, social studies, and math. Finally, we explained the critical role of families in children's literacy development and suggested ways of promoting successful partnerships between parents and teachers.

A child who does not have a well-developed vocabulary by age 3 can be considered at risk for poor achievement in school. The good news is that these children can catch up on their language development if they attend a high-quality preschool with an emphasis on language and literacy development (Barnett, 1995; Campbell & Raney, 1995). Teachers in these preschools purposefully and intentionally read to children, discuss books, and encourage children to use literacy in play. Children develop phonological awareness as they clap syllables in words and chant rhymes. Children who have quality preschool experiences are more likely to achieve throughout their education than are children who don't attend preschool (Hart & Risley, 1999). Children who attend preschool are less likely to be retained in the primary grades, have higher graduation rates from high school, and have fewer behavior problems. It is important that all children have a chance for literacy success by attending preschool (Barnett, 1995; Campbell & Raney, 1995).

Reading to children is one of the best and most familiar means of modeling literacy and exposing children to new language. These reading experiences must be accompanied by interactive discussions if children are to learn new vocabulary and language structures.

Teaching in preschool must be purposeful and intentional; we must establish and accomplish specific objectives. We can't leave instruction to spontaneous learning alone. The preschool years are precious and set the foundation for later success in school. Children from all backgrounds are likely to become successful readers and writers when they have well-prepared preschool teachers. They also need a program that focuses on language and literacy with concern for social, emotional, physical and cognitive development; and a strong family involvement component. With knowledge of genres and effective teaching strategies to enhance understanding of text, teachers can help children to read successfully and motivate them to become lifelong voluntary readers.

Recommended Children's Literature

This appendix contains lists of different types of children's books—organized by genre—that can be introduced to preschool children, as well as a list of magazines.

Alphabet Books

Andreae, G. (2003). *K is for kissing a cool kangaroo*. New York: Scholastic.

Diaz, J., & Gerth, M. (2003). *My first jumbo book of letters*. New York: Scholastic.

Horenstein, H. (1999). *Arf! beg! catch! Dogs from a to z*. New York: Scholastic.

Isadora, R. (2001). *ABC pop*. New York: Penguin.

Kirk, D. (2002). *Miss Spider's ABC*. Lexington, KY: Book Wholesalers.

Mazollo, J. (2000). *I spy little letters*. New York: Scholastic.

Whitehouse, P. (2002). *Food ABC: The colors we eat*. Chicago: Heinemann.

Whitford, P. (2001). *Everything to spend the night from A to Z*. New York: Scholastic.

Books About Realistic Issues

Alexander, M. (2006). *Nobody asked me if I wanted a baby sister*. Watertown, MA: Charlesbridge.

Brandt, A. (2004). *When Katie was our teacher*. St. Paul, MN: Redleaf.

Davis, K. (2002). *I hate to go to bed*. San Diego, CA: Harcourt.

Hale, I. (1992). *How I found a friend*. New York: Viking.

Lindsay, J.W. (2000). *Do I have a daddy?* Buena Park, CA: Morning Glory.

Maynard, B. (1999). *Quiet, Wyatt!* New York: Penguin.

Numeroff, L.J. (2001). *What grandmas do best/what grandpas do best*. New York: Simon & Schuster.

Palatini, M. (2000). *Good as Goldie*. New York: Hyperion.

Shannon, D. (1999). *David goes to school*. New York: Scholastic.

Books Related to Cultural Diversity

Adoff, A. (2004). *Black is brown is tan*. New York: HarperCollins.

Ashley, B. (1995). *Cleversticks*. New York: Crown.

Avery, C.E. (2004). *Everybody has feelings*. Beltsville, MD: Gryphon House.

Baer, E. (1992). *This is the way we go to school: A book about children around the world*. New York: Scholastic.

Dorros, A. (1997). *Abuela*. New York: Puffin.

Hamanaka, S. (1999). *All the colors of the Earth*. New York: HarperCollins.

Hoffman, M. (1998). *Amazing Grace*. New York: Penguin.

Lin, G. (2004). *Kite flying*. New York: Random House.

Lind, M. (2003). *Bluebonnet girl*. New York: Henry Holt.

London, J. (2000). *Who bop?* New York: HarperCollins.

Montanari, D. (2004). *Children around the world*. Tonawanda, NY: Kids Can Press.

Morris, A. (1993). *Hats, hats, hats*. New York: HarperCollins.

Peacock, C.A. (2004). *Mommy far, mommy near: An adoption story*. Morton Grove, IL: Albert Whitman.

Strickland, D.S., & Strickland, M.R. (1996). *Families: Poems celebrating the African-American experience*. Honesdale, PA: Boyds Mills Press.

van Dort, E. (1998). *Am I really different?* Edinburgh, Scotland: Floris.

Watlington, C. (2002). *Zoe*. Emcor, Nicaragua: Ebonylaw.

Woodson, J. (2001). *The other side*. New York: Penguin.

Cardboard Concept Books

Barrett, J.E. (2000). *Too big for diapers: Featuring Jim Henson's Sesame Street Muppets*. New York: Random House.

Carle, E. (2005). *Does a kangaroo have a mother, too?* New York: HarperCollins.

Deschamps, N. (2003). *Things that go*. New York: DK Publishing.

Dr. Seuss. (2003). *Happy birthday to you: A pop-up book*. New York: Random House.

Martin, B., Jr. (2006). *Panda bear, panda bear, what do you see?* New York: Holt.

Tracy, T. (1999). *Show me!* New York: HarperCollins.

Classic Picture Storybooks

Barrett, J. (1988). *Animals should definitely not wear clothing*. New York: Simon & Schuster.

Bemelmans, L. (1998). *Madeline*. Cambridge, MA: Schoenhof Foreign Books.

Berenstain, S., & Berenstain, J. (1966). *The bear's picnic*. New York: Random House.

Bourgeois, P. (1997). *Franklin in the dark*. Toronto, ON: Kids Can Press.

Brown, M.W. (2005). *Goodnight moon*. New York: HarperCollins.

Carle, E. (2007). *The very hungry caterpillar*. New York: Penguin.

dePaola, T. (1979). *Strega Nona*. New York: Simon & Schuster.

Eastman, P.D. (2005). *Are you my mother?* New York: Random House.

Flack, M. (1999). *Ask Mr. Bear*. Orlando, FL: Harcourt School.

Hoban, R. (1976). *Best friends for Frances*. New York: HarperCollins.

Hutchins, P. (1994). *Don't forget the bacon*. New York: HarperCollins.

Johnson, C. (1981). *Harold and the purple crayon*. New York: HarperCollins.

Keats, E.J. (1998). *The snowy day*. New York: Puffin.

Kellogg, S. (1992). *Can I keep him?* New York: Penguin.

Kraus, R. (1994). *Leo the late bloomer*. New York: HarperCollins.

Lionni, L. (2005). *Swimmy*. Germany: Beltz & Gelberg.

McCloskey, R. (1976). *Blueberries for Sal*. New York: Penguin.

Piper, W. (2005). *The little engine that could* (Reillustrated ed.). New York: Penguin.

Potter, B. (2002). *The tale of Peter Rabbit*. New York: Penguin.

Sendak, M. (1991). *Where the wild things are*. New York: HarperCollins.

Slobodkina, E. (1987). *Caps for sale*. New York: HarperCollins.

Viorst, J. (1987). *Alexander and the terrible, horrible, no good, very bad day*. New York: Simon & Schuster.

Waber, B. (1975). *Ira sleeps over*. Boston: Houghton Mifflin.

Cloth Books

Cousins, L. (1992). *Flower in the garden*. Cambridge, MA: Candlewick.

Cousins, L. (1992). *Hen on the farm*. Cambridge, MA: Candlewick.

Kunhardt, D.M.. (2003). *Sleepy bunny*. New York: Golden.

Kueffner, S. (1999). *Look, baby!* New York: Friedman-Fairfax.

Rettore, A.S. (2004). *Lucky ladybug*. New York: Cartwheel.

Concept Books

Backpack Books. (2002). *It's about time!* (Huggy Buggy series). New York: Barnes and Noble.

Davis, K. (2001). *Soft shapes: On and off*. Norwalk, CT: Innovative Kids.

Hoban, T. (1987). *I read signs*. New York: HarperCollins.

Hoban, T. (1998). *More, fewer, less*. New York: Greenwillow.

Klingel, C., & Noyed, R.B. (2001). *Pigs*. Chanhassen, MI: The Child's World.

Miller, M. (1998). *Big and little*. New York: Greenwillow.

Murphy, C. (2000). *Black cat, white cat: A book of opposites*. New York: Simon & Schuster.

Nonfiction Books

Maass, R. (1996). *When summer comes*. New York: Holt.

Macken, J.E. (2003). *Crossing guard*. Milwaukee, WI: Gareth Stevens.

Reid, M.E. (1997). *Let's find out about ice cream*. New York: Scholastic.

Rotner, S. (2000). *The body book*. New York: Orchard.

Satoh, A., & Toda, K. (2000). *Animal faces*. New York: Kane/Miller.

Saunders-Smith, G. (1998). *The fire station*. Mankato, MN: Pebble.

Saunders-Smith, G. (2000). *Flowers*. Mankato, MN: Pebble.

Number Books

Baker, A. (1998). *Little rabbit's first number book*. Boston: Houghton Mifflin.

Bang, M. (1996). *Ten, nine, eight*. New York: Tupelo.

Beaton, C. (2002). *One moose, twenty mice*. Cambridge, MA: Barefoot Books.

Carle, E. (2007). *1, 2, 3 to the zoo*. New York: Penguin.

Christelow, E. (2006). *Five little monkeys jumping on the bed*. Boston: Houghton Mifflin.

Ehlert, L. (2001). *Fish eyes: A book you can count on*. San Diego, CA: Harcourt.

Falconer, I. (2002). *Olivia counts*. New York: Atheneum.

Gerth, M. (2006). *Ten little ladybugs*. Atlanta: Piggy Toes Press.

Hubbard, P. (1999). *Trick or treat countdown*. New York: Holiday House.

Miranda, A. (2002). *Monster math*. San Diego, CA: Harcourt.

Strickland, P. (2000). *Ten terrible dinosaurs*. New York: Puffin.

Nursery Rhymes

Opie, I.A. (Ed.). (1996). *My very first Mother Goose*. Cambridge, MA: Candlewick.

Scarry, R. (1999). *Best Mother Goose ever*. New York: Golden.

Wright, B.F. (2007). *The real mother goose*. Champaign, IL: Book Jungle.

Plastic Books

Aigner-Clark, J. (2003). *Baby Einstein: Water, water everywhere*. New York: Hyperion.

Bevington, K. (2002). *A frog's life*. Brooklyn, NY: Straight Edge Press.

Hill, E. (2003). *Spot goes splash*. New York: Putnam.

London, J. (2001). *Froggy takes a bath*. New York: Grosset & Dunlap.

Potter, B. (2002). *The tale of Benjamin Bunny*. New York: Frederick Warne.

Poetry

Bierhorst, J. (Ed.). (1998). *In the trail of the wind: American Indian poems and ritual orations*. New York: Farrar, Straus and Giroux.

Feldman, T. (2003). *First foil poetry haikus: Love*. Los Angeles: Piggy Toes Press.

Florian, D. (2004). *Mammalabilia*. San Diego, CA: Harcourt.

Hoberman, M. (2007). *You read to me, I'll read to you*. New York: Little, Brown.

Kuskin, K. (2003). *Moon, have you met my mother? The collected poems of Karla Kuskin*. New York: HarperCollins.

Prelutsky, J. (1999). *The 20th century children's poetry treasury*. New York: Random House.

Predictable Books

Repetitive Phrases

Chapman, C. (1994). *Snow on snow on snow*. New York: Dial.

Sendak, M. (1991). *Chicken soup with rice*. New York: HarperCollins.

Wilson, K., & Rankin, J. (2003). *A frog in the bog*. New York: Simon & Schuster.

Rhyme

Alborough, J. (2008). *Duck in the truck*. La Jolla, CA: Kane/Miller.

Ashman, L. (2002). *Can you make a piggy giggle?* New York: Dutton.

Beaton, C. (2004). *How big is a pig?* Cambridge, MA: Barefoot Books.

Christelow, E. (2004). *Five little monkeys wash the car*. Boston: Houghton Mifflin.

Dr. Seuss. (1960). *Green eggs and ham*. New York: Random House.

Fleming, D. (2005). *Pumpkin eye*. New York: Henry Holt.

Kuskin, K. (1995). *James and the rain*. New York: Simon & Schuster.

McMillan, B. (2001). *Puffins climb, penguins rhyme*. San Diego, CA: Harcourt.

Newcome, Z. (2002). *Head, shoulders, knees and toes and other action rhymes*. Cambridge, MA: Candlewick.

Schotter, R. (2000). *Captain Bob sets sail*. New York: Atheneum.

Familiar Sequences

Carlstrom, N.W. (1999). *How do you say it today, Jesse Bear?* New York: Aladdin.

Carlstrom, N.W. (2005). *Jesse Bear, what will you wear?* New York: Aladdin.

Hubbard, P. (1999). *Trick or treat countdown*. New York: Holiday House.

Updike, J. (1999). *A child's calendar*. New York: Holiday House.

Van Allsburg, C. (1998). *The z was zapped*. Boston: Houghton Mifflin.

Cumulative Patterns

Carle, E. (2000). *The very lonely firefly*. New York: Penguin.

Tompert, A. (1996). *Just a little bit*. Boston: Houghton Mifflin.

Wood, A. (1994). *The napping house wakes up*. San Diego, CA: Harcourt.

Theme Books

Animals and Insects

Barton, B. (2001). *Dinosaurs, dinosaurs*. New York: HarperCollins.

Collard, S.B. (2000). *Animal dads*. Boston: Houghton Mifflin.

Glaser, L. (1994). *Wonderful worms*. Minneapolis, MN: Lerner.

Hurd, E.T. (2000). *Starfish*. New York: Scholastic.

Klingel, C.F. , & Noyed, R.B. (2001). *Pigs*. Chanhassen, MI: Child's World.

Nicholson, S. (1999). *A day at Greenhill farm*. New York: DK Publishing.

Rockwell, A.F. (2001). *Bugs are insects*. New York: HarperCollins.

Selsam, M.E. (1995). *How to be a nature detective*. New York: HarperCollins.

Human Body

Carle, E. (1999). *From head to toe*. New York: HarperCollins.

Cole, J. (1993). *The magic school bus: Inside the human body*. New York: Scholastic.

Hewitt, S. (1999). *The five senses*. New York: Children's Press.

Kates, B.J. (1996). *Sesame Street: We're different, we're the same*. New York: Random House.

Sakelaris, P. (2000). *Giggle belly*. New York: Children's Press.

Serfozo, M. (2000). *A head is for hats*. New York: Scholastic.

Shappie, T.L. (1997). *Where is your nose?* New York: Scholastic.

Nutrition

Frost, H. (2000). *The dairy group*. Mankato, MN: Capstone.

Katzen, M., & Henderson, A. (2004). *Pretend soup and other real recipes: A cookbook for preschoolers and up*. Berkeley, CA: Ten Speed Press.

Robinson, F. (1995). *Vegetables, vegetables*. San Francisco: Children's Book Press.

Royston, A. (2002). *Eat well*. London: Heinemann.

Silverstein, A., Silverstein, V.B., & Silverstein Nunn, L. (2000). *Eat your vegetables! Drink your milk!* New York: Scholastic.

Whitehouse, P. (2002). *Food ABC*. London: Heinemann.

William, M. (2002). *Eat healthy, feel great*. Boston: Little, Brown.

Plants

Carle, E. (2005). *The tiny seed*. New York: Simon & Schuster.

Cole, H. (1997). *Jack's garden*. New York: HarperCollins.

Ehlert, L. (2003). *Planting a rainbow*. San Diego, CA: Harcourt.

Ehlert, L. (2004). *Growing vegetable soup*. San Diego, CA: Harcourt.

Klingel, C., & Noyed, R.B. (2000). *Pumpkins*. Chanhassen, MI: Child's World.

Rockwell, A. (1999). *One bean*. Thornton, NH: Walker & Co.

Safety

Cuyler, M. (2004). *Stop, drop, and roll*. Pine Plains, NY: Live Oak Media.

Raatma, L. (2004). *Safety on the playground*. Mankato, MN: Child's World.

Thomas, P. (2003). *I can be safe*. Hauppauge, NY: Barrons.

Weather and Seasons

Backpack Books. (2002). *What's the weather?* New York: Barnes and Noble.

Blackstone, S. (2004). *Bear in sunshine*. Cambridge, MA: Barefoot Books.

Branley, F. (2000). *Snow is falling*. New York: HarperCollins.

Saunders, G. (2000). *Autumn*. Mankato, MN: Coughlan.

Shaw, C. (1988). *It looked like spilt milk*. New York: HarperCollins.

Siddals, M.M. (2001). *Tell me a season*. Boston: Houghton Mifflin.

Touch-and-Feel Books

Boynton, S. (1998). *Dinosaur's binkit*. New York: Little Simon.

Kunhardt, D. (2001). *Pat the Bunny* series. New York: Random House.

Pledger, M. (2001). *In the ocean*. San Diego, CA: Silver Dolphin.

Saltzberg, B. (2000). *Animal kisses*. San Diego, CA: Harcourt.

Watt, F., & Wells, R. (2004). *That's not my dinosaur*. Tulsa, OK: EDC Publishing.

Traditional Literature: Fairy Tales, Fables, Myths, and Folk Tales

Asbjornsen, P.C., & Moe, J.E. (1991). *The three billy goats gruff*. San Diego, CA: Harcourt.

Brett, J. (1996). *Goldilocks and the three bears*. New York: Putnam.

Capucilli, A.S. (2006). *Biscuit goes to school*. New York: Barnes and Noble.

Galdone, P. (1983). *The gingerbread man*. Boston: Houghton Mifflin.

Galdone, P. (1985). *The little red hen*. Boston: Houghton Mifflin.

Bilingual Books

Beinstein, P., & Thompson Bros. (2003). *Dora's book of words/Libro de palabras de Dora: A bilingual pull-tab adventure!* New York: Simon Spotlight/Nickelodeon.

Betrand, D.G. (2008). *My pal, Victor/Mi amigo, Victor*. McHenry, IL: Raven Tree Press.

Bridwell, N. (2003). *Clifford's bathtime/Clifford i la hora del bano*. New York: Scholastic.

Pandell, K. (2003). *I love you sun, I love you moon/Te amo sol, Te amo luna*. New York: Putnam Juvenile.

Pfister, M. (2006). *Rainbow Fish opposites/opuestos*. New York: North-South.

Reiser, L. (1996). *Margaret and Margarita/Margarita y Margaret*. New York: Rayo/Harper Collins.

Schumacher, B. (2006). *Body parts/Las partes del cuerpo*. Racine, WI: Learning Props.

Valeri, M.E. (2006). *The hare and the tortoise/La liebrey la tortuga*. San Francisco: Chronicle Books.

Multicultural Books

Castaneda, O. (1995). *Abuela's weave*. New York: Lee & Low.

Dooley, N. (1992). *Everybody cooks rice*. Minneapolis, MN: Carolrhoda.

Friedman, I.R. (1987). *How my parents learned to eat*. Boston: Sandpiper Houghton Mifflin.

Heide, F.P. (1995). *The day of Ahmed's secret*. New York: HarperTrophy.

Ho, M. (1996). *Hush! A Thai lullaby*. New York: Orchard.

Lee, H.V. (1999). *At the beach*. Topeka, KS: Topeka Bindery.

Onyefulu, I. (1997). *A is for Africa*. New York: Puffin.

Magazines

Nick Jr.
Nick Jr. magazine provides activities for kids ages 2–6 including the latest information on child development, news, and family products sure to be appreciated by parents and teachers.

Zoobooks
Every monthly issue contains color illustrations, diagrams, and photos about a featured animal that is both educational and entertaining.

Highlights High Five
Highlights High Five was created to encourage young children's development. Based on sound educational principles and widely accepted child-development theories, each monthly issue brings a 40-page, high-quality mix of read-aloud stories and age-appropriate puzzles and activities.

National Geographic Kids
This magazine features stories on animals, science, technology, and accomplishments of kids around the world. Puzzles, games, posters, and trading cards are also included.

Disney and Me Magazine
Brings readers a classic children's favorite. Featuring Winnie the Pooh and friends for early learning fun in a bi-monthly, full size, 32-page children's magazine for ages 2–6. Each issue includes stories, drawing, matching, counting, coloring, and a pull-out workbook.

Your Big Back Yard Magazine
A publication of the National Wildlife Federation, written for kids ages 3–5. Each issue sparks a child's natural curiosity and interest in reading as it introduces them to the world of nature with photos of baby animals, read-to-me stories, poems, riddles, and games.

Ladybug Magazine
Filled with characters, games, songs, poems, and stories for children ages 2–6.

Preschool Playroom Magazine
Written for preschoolers and kindergarteners, featuring drawing, counting, coloring and reading activities, with a character poster and a six-page pull-out workbook in every issue. "Playroom pen pals" page encourages children to write in or draw pictures of their favorite characters.

Thomas and Friends Magazine
Brings to life the magical world of Thomas and his friends for early learners. Every issue is filled with stories and includes a collectible poster, educational activities, and a pull-out workbook.

Recommended New and Alternative Literacies

Websites

The McGraw-Hill Website for Children's Literature
www.mhhe.com/socscience/education/kidlit/
A database of children's literature, online lesson plans, and activities to implement in the classroom, as well as featured authors and books of the month.

Preschool at The Literacy Web
www.literacy.uconn.edu/pkhome.htm
A literacy web resource page that includes easy access to a wide assortment of literacy ideas customized for use by preschoolers and their teachers.

Read With Me!
www.teachersandfamilies.com/open/psreading.cfm
A list of must-read books for preschoolers.

Books and Literature Preschool Activities and Crafts
www.first-school.ws/theme/books.htm
Activities and art projects to reinforce comprehension of children's literature in preschool classrooms.

Carol Hurst's Children's Literature Site
www.carolhurst.com/titles/prek.html
A list of reviewed children's literature for preschoolers.

International Children's Digital Library
www.icdlbooks.org/
An international children's digital library meant to excite and inspire the world's children to become members of the global community by making the best in children's literature available online.

Television Shows Based on Children's Literature

Arthur

This story is about an aardvark and his interactions with peers and family. The series often deals with social and health-related issues that affect young children. There is also a strong emphasis on the educational value of books and libraries.

Clifford the Big Red Dog

The runt of the litter, Clifford was chosen by a city child named Emily Elizabeth Howard as her birthday present. Clifford grew to over 25 feet tall, forcing the family to leave the city and move to an open suburb.

Berenstain Bears

A family of bears living in Bear Country deals with topics relevant to family life.

Curious George

A curious chimpanzee named George leaves his home in Africa to live with "The Man with The Yellow Hat" in a big city. An animated television series was developed from the book's plot and characters.

Winnie the Pooh

The lovable bear Winnie the Pooh and his master, Christopher Robin, and friends have many fun adventures taking place in the Hundred Acre Wood. The show brings alive the humor and excitement of the original books.

Little Bear

Little Bear is a grizzly bear cub, who gets into trouble and has wonderful adventures with his other animal friends. The show teaches children about emotions and feelings, and how to deal with them as shown through the relatable characters.

The Magic School Bus

Ms. Frizzle and her class board a magical school bus that takes them on field trips to places of great imagination. This bus can also transform into a spaceship, a boat, and an animal. The show aims to teach children about science through an interactive approach.

Madeline
In 1930s France, little Madeline and her friends go happily about their daily lives. She displays bravery and kindness in the face of difficulty.

Storytelling Ideas for Developing Comprehension

This appendix contains stories that emphasize specific storytelling techniques for teachers to use with their children—sound story, chalk talk, origami story, and prop story.

Sound Story

Sample Story: "The Grouchy Queen and the Happy King"
(adapted from an anonymous tale)

When the underlined words are mentioned, the following sounds are made:

> *<u>Queen Grace the Grouch</u>: Grrrrr.*
>
> *<u>King Happy Herman</u>: Ha-ha-ha.*
>
> *<u>Whistling Wilbur</u>: Whistling sound high to low.*
>
> *<u>Singing Sam</u>: La-la-la (first few notes of "Mary Had a Little Lamb").*
>
> *<u>Tired Tim</u>: Ahhhh (yawning sound).*
>
> *<u>Lively Lorraine</u>: Ah ha.*

Once upon a time there was a queen named <u>Grace the Grouch</u>. She had this name because she growled most of the time. <u>Queen Grace the Grouch</u> was married to <u>King Happy Herman</u>. He was called <u>Happy Herman</u> because he laughed most of the time. Together they made a perfect couple. <u>Queen Grace the Grouch</u> and <u>King Happy Herman</u> had three sons. The first son's name was <u>Whistling Wilbur</u>. He had this name because he whistled almost all the time. The second son's name was <u>Singing Sam</u>. He had this name because most of the time he sang. The third son's name was <u>Tired Tim</u>. He had this name because most of the time he was sleeping, and when he was awake he was doing almost nothing but yawning.

There was a princess from the next kingdom named <u>Lively Lorraine</u>. She couldn't sit still for a moment. She bounced around from dawn till dusk looking for things to do. Each time the princess would find a job to be done, she'd lift her hand in the air and say, "Ah ha." When most people spoke of Lorraine, they could not help but say, "Ah ha."

<u>Lively Lorraine</u> decided that she'd like to marry. She knew of <u>Queen Grace the Grouch</u> and her husband, <u>King Happy Herman</u>. She also knew about their three sons, <u>Whistling Wilbur</u>, <u>Singing Sam</u>, and <u>Tired Tim</u>. <u>Lively Lorraine</u> decided to take a look at the three princes to see if one might be a suitable future king for her. She saddled her horse one day and away she galloped to the kingdom over the hill.

When she arrived, she was greeted by <u>Queen Grace the Grouch</u> and her husband, <u>King Happy Herman</u>. <u>Lively Lorraine</u> decided to stay a while to get to know each prince and to see if there was one that best suited her.

First, <u>Lively Lorraine</u> played tennis with <u>Whistling Wilbur</u>. But he whistled so much throughout the game that <u>Lively Lorraine</u> could not concentrate and kept missing the ball.

The next day, Lorraine went sailing with <u>Singing Sam</u>. Sam was nice, but he never stopped singing. Instead of talking, he'd find an appropriate song and sing what he had to say. For a while it was fun, but Lorraine tired of it quickly.

<u>Lively Lorraine</u> felt sad. She decided that she would not meet the prince of her dreams here in this kingdom. But suddenly, <u>Tired Tim</u> came yawning down the garden path. Lorraine took one look at him an said, "Ah Ha." Somehow <u>Lively Lorraine</u> and <u>Tired Tim</u> made the perfect couple—something like <u>Queen Grace the Grouch</u> and <u>King Happy Herman</u>.

So <u>Lively Lorraine</u> and <u>Tired Tim</u> trotted off to the kingdom over the hill to be married. Of course, they lived happily ever after.

Chalk Talk

Sample Story: "The Surprise in the Playhouse" (adapted from an anonymous tale)

In this story, the underlined words indicate when to draw.

There was once a little girl named Lori, and there is an <u>L</u> for Lori. Lori found a great big empty refrigerator box one day outside a neighbor's house; it was left for the garbage man to pick up. Lori decided that the refrigerator box would make a terrific playhouse. She dragged the box home and set it in her backyard, and it looked <u>like this.</u>

The house needed a lot of work. The first thing Lori did was to <u>cut out two squares to make windows</u>, like this. Then she drew some <u>pretty shutters</u> that looked like these.

When she finished with the windows, <u>she cut out a door</u> just like this.

Lori wanted a way to get in and out of her house from the back. She thought about it a while and decided to make the back all open so it would feel bigger inside and a lot of light could shine in. To do this, <u>she cut the sides of the box, on both sides, down the middle and pulled the flaps open.</u> It made the house look like this.

Lori found some tiny garden fencing in her garage. <u>She put the fence in front of her playhouse</u> and planted seeds behind the fence.

Now that her house was finished, she thought she'd go get her friend Linda. That's another <u>L</u> for Linda.

Linda lived across the street and down the block. So Lori skipped <u>across the street and went down the block</u> to Linda's house. <u>She went to the front door</u> and rang the bell.

Linda's mother came to the door and said that Linda was upstairs in her room playing. <u>So Lori went upstairs</u> and asked Linda if she would like to see her new playhouse.

Linda said yes, so the <u>two girls hurried down the stairs.</u> Linda forgot her sweater so <u>she ran back up again</u> to get it. Now the girls were ready to go. <u>They went across the street</u> and were on their way back to Lori's house.

Lori stopped a minute and <u>bent down to look</u> at a caterpillar. Linda looked, too. <u>The girls got up and hurried along.</u> Then they pretended they were bunnies and <u>jumped up and down as they went. Lori fell down and Linda helped her up.</u>

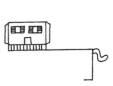
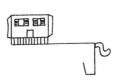
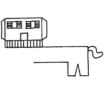
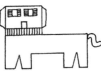

Origami Story

Sample Story: *Swimmy*
by Leo Lionni (2005)

A little black fish escapes being eaten by a giant tuna and finds comfort and safety in numbers with his new friends. Origami technique: Fold paper into the shape of a fish.

Activity

1. Practice folding origami figures until you feel confident with the technique and can fold and tell the story smoothly.
2. While telling the story, fold the paper into the main character or object and display it until the story is ended.

Origami Fish

Enlarge as needed. Fold as indicated in order by number.

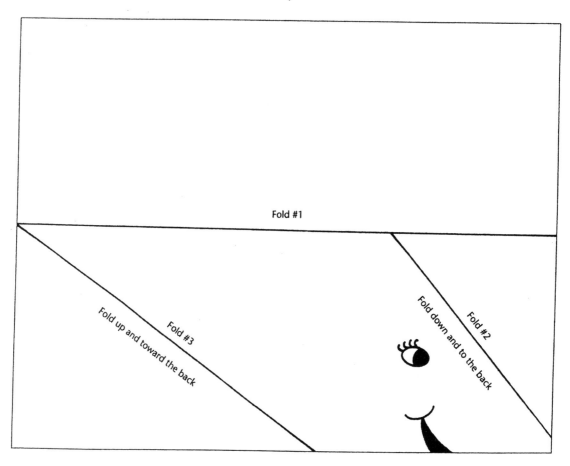

Prop Story

Sample Story: "The Little Round Red House"
(adapted from an anonymous tale)

School had ended for the summer. Stephanie was wandering around the house trying to find something to do. She colored for a while, cut and pasted, and looked at some books, but nothing seemed like much fun. She looked for her mother. Her mother was at her desk, busy with some important work.

Stephanie said to her mother, "What can I do today? I just can't seem to find anything."

Her mother thought for a while and said, "Stephanie, I know what you can do. Go outside for a walk and see if you can find a little round red house that has no windows and no doors, a chimney on top, and a star inside."

Stephanie wasn't really sure what her mother was talking about, but since it sounded interesting she decided to give it a try. First, Stephanie walked down Elm Street. Then she tried Heritage Lane, but not one house fit the description her mother had given. She could not find a little round red house that had no windows and no doors, a chimney on top, and a star inside. All the houses had windows and doors. None of the houses was even red.

When she was about to give up and go home, she met her friend Darren. He was looking for something to do. Stephanie asked him to help her with her search. The two children decided to ask Mr. and Mrs. Mandel if they knew of this little round red house. Mr. and Mrs. Mandel owned the candy shop, and they knew everything about the town in which Stephanie and Darren lived. If anyone would know about such a strange house, it would be the Mandels.

Stephanie ran into the candy shop. She immediately asked Mrs. Mandel if she knew of a little round red house that had no windows and no doors, a chimney on top, and a star inside. Mrs. Mandel thought for a while and then said, "Stephanie, go down to the shady pond where the wind blows through the trees. Sit down a while to enjoy the summer day and the breeze rippling through the trees, and maybe you will find what you are looking for."

Darren and Stephanie hurried down to the shady pond. It was a long walk and the day was hot, so they were happy to sit down and rest by the pond in the shade of the trees. Before long, a lovely cool breeze blew through the branches of the trees. The leaves rustled, and something fell out of one of the trees.

Whatever fell bounded first on Stephanie's head and then fell to the ground. It had split into two pieces. Stephanie picked up the two pieces and put them back together again. Then she began to laugh. "My goodness," she said, "I've found it! This is the little round red house that has no windows and no doors, a chimney on top, and a star inside." Hungry from their experience, Darren and Stephanie each took a piece and enjoyed the apple [*show cut apple*] that had fallen from the tree.

Cut apple on the dotted line.

REFERENCES

Anderson, R.C., Hiebert, E.H., Scott, J.A., & Wilkinson, I.A.G. (1985). *Becoming a nation of readers: The report of the Commission on Reading*. Washington, DC: National Institute of Education.

Applebee, A.N., Langer, J.A., & Mullis, I.V.S. (1988). *Who reads best? Factors related to reading achievement in grades 3, 7, and 11.* Princeton, NJ: Educational Testing Service.

Barnett, W.S. (1995). Long-term effects of early childhood programs on cognitive and school outcomes. *The Future of Children, 5*(3), 25–50. doi:10.2307/1602366

Baumann, J.F., Seifert-Kessell, N., & Jones, L.A. (1992). Effect of think-aloud instruction on elementary students' comprehension monitoring abilities. *Journal of Reading Behavior, 24*(2), 143–172.

Burns, M.S., Griffin, P., & Snow, C.E. (Eds.). (1999). *Starting out right: A guide to promoting children's reading success.* Washington, DC: National Academy Press.

Bus, A.G., van IJzendoorn, M.H., & Pellegrini, A.D. (1995). Joint book reading makes for success in learning to read: A meta-analysis in intergenerational transmission of literacy. *Review of Educational Research, 65*(1), 1–21.

Campbell, F.A., & Raney, C.T. (1995). Cognitive and school outcomes for high-risk African-American students in middle adolescence: Positive effects of early intervention. *American Educational Research Journal, 32*(4), 743–772.

Clark, M.M. (1984). Literacy at home and at school: Insights from a study of young fluent readers. In J. Goelman, A.A. Oberg, & F. Smith (Eds.), *Awaking to literacy* (pp. 122–130). Portsmouth, NH: Heinemann.

Cochran-Smith, M. (1984). *The making of a reader.* Norwood, NJ: Ablex.

Cosgrove, M.S. (1989). Read out loud? Why bother? *New England Reading Association Journal, 25,* 9–22.

Cullinan, B.E. (Ed.). (1987). *Children's literature in the reading program.* Newark, DE: International Reading Association.

Cullinan, B.E. (Ed.). (1992). *Invitation to read: More children's literature in the reading program.* Newark, DE: International Reading Association.

Edwards, P.A. (1995). Combining parents' and teachers' thoughts about storybook reading at home and school. In L.M. Morrow (Ed.), *Family literacy: Connections in schools and communities* (pp. 54–69). Newark, DE: International Reading Association.

Elley, W.B. (1989). Vocabulary acquisition from listening to stories. *Reading Research Quarterly, 24*(2), 174–187. doi:10.2307/747863

Fisher, D., Flood, J., & Lapp, D. (1999). The role of literature in literacy development. In L.B. Gambrell, L.M. Morrow, S.B. Neuman, & M. Pressley (Eds.), *Best practices in literacy instruction* (pp. 119–135). New York: Guilford.

Fountas, I.C., & Pinnell, G.S. (1996). *Guided reading: Good first teaching for all children.* Portsmouth, NH: Heinemann.

Gambrell, L.B., & Koskinen, P.S. (2002). Imagery: A strategy for enhancing comprehension. In C.C. Block & M. Pressley (Eds.), *Comprehension instruction: Research-based best practices* (pp. 305–319). New York: Guilford.

Gambrell, L.B., Pfeiffer, W.R, & Wilson, R.M. (1985). The effect of retelling upon reading comprehension and recall of text information. *The Journal of Educational Research, 78*(4), 216–220.

Glazer, J.I. (1991). *Literature for young children* (3rd ed.). New York: Merrill.

Graves, M.F., Juel, C., & Graves, B.B. (1998). *Teaching reading in the 21st century.* Boston: Allyn & Bacon.

Guthrie, J.T. (2002). Engagement and motivation in reading instruction. In M.L. Kamil, J.B. Manning, & H.J. Walberg (Eds.), *Successful reading instruction* (pp. 137–154). Greenwich, CT: Information Age.

Hannon, P. (1995). *Literacy, home and school: Research and practice in teaching literacy with parents.* London: Falmer.

Hart, B., & Risley, T.R. (1999). *The social world of children learning to talk.* Baltimore: Paul H. Brookes.

Heath, S.B. (1982). What no bedtime story means: Narrative skills at home and school. *Language in Society, 11*(1), 49–76.

Holdaway, D. (1979). *The foundations of literacy.* Sydney: Ashton Scholastic.

Huck, C.S. (1992). Books for emergent readers. In B.E. Cullinan (Ed.), *Invitation to read: More children's literature in the reading program* (pp. 2–13). Newark, DE: International Reading Association.

Kuhn, M.R., & Stahl, S.A. (2003). Fluency: A review of developmental and remedial practices. *Journal of Educational Psychology, 95*(1), 3–21. doi:10.1037/0022-0663.95.1.3

Leichter, H.P. (1984). Families as environments for literacy. In H. Goelman, A.A. Oberg, & F. Smith (Eds.), *Awakening to literacy* (pp. 38–50). Portsmouth, NH: Heinemann.

Manning, M.M., Manning, G.L., & Long, R. (1994). *Theme immersion: Inquiry-based curriculum in elementary and middle schools.* Portsmouth, NH: Heinemann.

Martinez, M., & Teale, W.H. (1988). Reading in a kindergarten classroom library. *The Reading Teacher, 41*(6), 568–573.

McKenna, M.C. (2001). Development of reading attitudes. In L. Verhoeven & C. Snow (Eds.), *Literacy and motivation: Reading engagement in individuals and groups* (pp. 135–158). Mahwah, NJ: Erlbaum.

Miramontes, O.B., Nadeau, A., & Commins, N.C. (1997). *Restructuring schools for linguistic diversity: Linking decision making to effective programs.* New York: Teachers College Press.

Morrow, L.M. (1982). Relationships between literature programs, library corner designs, and children's use of literature. *The Journal of Educational Research, 75*(6), 339–344.

Morrow, L.M. (1983). Home and school correlates of early interest in literature. *The Journal of Educational Research*, 76(4), 221–230.

Morrow, L.M. (1984). Reading stories to young children: Effects of story structure and traditional questioning strategies on comprehension. *Journal of Reading Behavior*, 16, 273–288.

Morrow, L.M. (1985). Retelling stories: A strategy for improving young children's comprehension, concept of story structure, and oral language complexity. *The Elementary School Journal*, 85(5), 646–661. doi:10.1086/461427

Morrow, L.M. (1986, December). *Promoting responses to literature: Children's responses to one-to-one story readings.* Paper presented at the 36th annual meeting of the National Reading Conference, Austin, TX.

Morrow, L.M. (1987). The effects of one-to-one story readings on children's questions and comments. In S. Baldwin & J. Readence (Eds.), *36th yearbook of the National Reading Conference* (pp. 75–84). Rochester, NY: National Reading Conference.

Morrow, L.M. (1988). Young children's responses to one-to-one story readings in school settings. *Reading Research Quarterly*, 23(1), 89–107. doi:10.2307/747906

Morrow, L.M. (1990). Preparing the classroom environment to promote literacy during play. *Early Childhood Research Quarterly*, 5(4), 537–554. doi:10.1016/0885-2006(90)90018-V

Morrow, L.M. (1992). The impact of a literature-based program on literacy achievement, use of literature, and attitudes of children from minority backgrounds. *Reading Research Quarterly*, 27(3), 250–275. doi:10.2307/747794

Morrow, L.M. (1996). Story retelling: A discussion strategy to develop and assess comprehension. In L.B. Gambrell & J.F. Almasi (Eds.), *Lively discussions! Fostering engaged reading* (pp. 265–285). Newark, DE: International Reading Association.

Morrow, L.M. (2005). *Literacy development in the early years: Helping children read and write* (5th ed.). Boston: Allyn & Bacon.

Morrow, L.M., O'Connor, E.M., & Smith, J.K. (1990). Effects of a story reading program on the literacy development of at-risk kindergarten children. *Journal of Reading Behavior*, 22(3), 255–275.

Moss, B., Leone, S., & Dipillo, M.L. (1997). Exploring the literature of fact: Linking reading and writing through information trade books. *Language Arts*, 74(6), 418–429.

National Institute of Child Health and Human Development. (2000). *Report of the National Reading Panel: Teaching children to read: An evidence-based assessment of the scientific research literature on reading and its implications for reading instruction* (NIH Publication No. 00-47690). Washington, DC: U.S. Government Printing Office.

Neuman, S.B., & Roskos, K.A. (1990). The influence of literacy-enriched play settings on preschoolers' engagement with written language. In J. Zutell & S. McCormick (Eds.), *Literacy theory and research: Analyses from multiple paradigms* (39th yearbook of the National Reading Conference, pp. 179–187). Chicago: National Reading Conference.

Neuman, S.B., & Roskos, K.A. (1993). *Language and literacy learning in the early years: An integrated approach.* Orlando, FL: Harcourt.

Ninio, A. (1980). Picture book reading in mother-infant dyads belonging to two subgroups in Israel. *Child Development, 51*(2), 587–590. doi:10.2307/1129299

Norton, D.E. (1999). *Through the eyes of a child: An introduction to children's literature* (5th ed.). Columbus, OH: Merrill.

Pappas, C.C., Kiefer, B.Z., & Levstik, L.S. (1995). *An integrated language perspective in the elementary school: Theory into action.* White Plains, NY: Longman.

Pearson, P.D., Roehler, L.R., Dole, J.A., & Duffy, G.G. (1992). Developing expertise in reading comprehension. In S.J. Samuels & A.E. Farsturp (Eds.), *What research has to say about reading instruction* (2nd ed., pp. 145–199). Newark, DE: International Reading Association.

Pellegrini, A.D., & Galda, L. (1982). The effects of thematic-fantasy play training on the development of children's story comprehension. *American Educational Research Journal, 19*(3), 443–452.

Pellegrini, A.D., Perlmutter, J.C., Galda, L., & Brody, G.H. (1990). Joint reading between black Head Start children and their mothers. *Child Development, 61*(2), 443–453. doi:10.2307/1131106

Pressley, M., & Afflerbach, P. (1995). *Verbal protocols of reading: The nature of constructively responsive reading.* Hillsdale, NJ: Erlbaum.

Pressley, M., & Hilden, K. (2002). How can children be taught to comprehend text better? In M.L. Kamil, J.B. Manning, & H.J. Walberg (Eds.), *Successful reading instruction* (pp. 33–53). Greenwich, CT: Information Age.

Rand, M.K. (1994). Using thematic instruction to organize an integrated language arts classroom. In L.M. Morrow, J.K. Smith, & L.C. Wilkinson (Eds.), *Integrated language arts: Controversy to consensus* (pp. 177–192). Boston: Allyn & Bacon.

RAND Reading Study Group. (2002). *Reading for understanding: Toward an R&D program in reading comprehension.* Santa Monica, CA: RAND.

Rasinski, T.V. (1990). Effects of repeated reading and listening-while-reading on reading fluency. *The Journal of Educational Research, 83*(3), 147–150.

Ritchie, S., James-Szanton, J., & Howes, C. (2002). Emergent literacy practices in early childhood classrooms. In C. Howes (Ed.), *Teaching 4- to 8-year-olds: Literacy, math, multiculturalism, and classroom community* (pp. 71–92). Baltimore: Paul H. Brookes.

Roser, N., & Martinez, M. (1985). Roles adults play in preschoolers' responses to literature. *Language Arts, 62*(5), 485–490.

Shaffer, D.R. (1989). *Developmental psychology: Childhood and adolescence* (2nd ed.). Pacific Grove, CA: Brooks/Cole.

Shore, K. (2001). Success for ESL students: 12 practical tips to help second language learners. *Instructor, 1*(110), 30–32, 106.

Stauffer, R.G. (1980). *The language-experience approach to the teaching of reading* (2nd ed.). New York: Harper & Row.

Sulzby, E. (1985). Children's emergent reading of favorite storybooks: A developmental study. *Reading Research Quarterly, 20*(4), 458–481. doi:10.1598/RRQ.20.4.4

Sulzby, E., & Teale, W.H. (1987). *Young children's storybook reading: Longitudinal study of parent–child interaction and children's independent functioning* (Final report to the Spencer Foundation). Ann Arbor: University of Michigan.

Taylor, D., & Strickland, D.S. (1986). *Family storybook reading.* Portsmouth, NH: Heinemann.

Teale, W.H. (1981). Parents reading to their children: What we know and need to know. *Language Arts, 58*(8), 902–912.

Teale, W.H., & Sulzby, E. (Eds.). (1986). *Emergent literacy: Writing and reading.* Norwood, NJ: Ablex.

Vukelich, C., Evans, C., & Albertson, B. (2003). Organizing expository texts: A look at the possibilities. In D.M. Barone & L.M. Morrow (Eds.), *Literacy and young children: Research-based practices* (pp. 261–290). New York: Guilford.

Walmsley, S.A. (1994). *Children exploring their world: Theme teaching in elementary school.* Portsmouth, NH: Heinemann.

Wepner, S.B., & Ray, L.C. (2000). Sign of the times: Technology and early literacy learning. In D.S. Strickland & L.M. Morrow (Eds.), *Beginning reading and writing* (pp. 168–182). New York: Teachers College Press; Newark, DE: International Reading Association.

Yopp, R.H., & Yopp, H.K. (2000). Sharing informational text with young children. *The Reading Teacher, 53*(5), 410–423.

CHILDREN'S LITERATURE CITED

Asbjornsen, P.C., & Moe, J.E. (1991). *The three billy goats gruff.* San Diego, CA: Harcourt.

Beall, P.C., & Nipp, S.H. (1989). *Wee sing, animals, animals, animals.* New York: Price Stern Sloan.

Bemelmans, L. (2000). *Madeline's rescue.* New York: Viking.

Bloom, S. (2007). *A splendid friend indeed.* Honesdale, PA: Boyds Mills.

Bourgeois, P. (1987). *Franklin in the dark.* Toronto, ON: Kids Can Press.

Brett, J. (1996). *Goldilocks and the three bears.* New York: Putnam.

Brown, M.W. (1989). *Big red barn.* New York: Scholastic.

Brown, M.W. (2005). *Goodnight moon.* New York: HarperCollins.

Cabrera, J. (2008). *Old McDonald had a farm.* New York: Holiday House.

Carle, E. (1989). *The very busy spider.* New York: Penguin.

Carle, E. (1994). *The very hungry caterpillar.* New York: Philomel.

Carle, E. (1998). *1, 2, 3 to the zoo: A counting book.* New York: Putnam.

Child, L. (1999). *Over the river and through the wood.* New York: Morrow.

Dr. Seuss. (1970). *Mr. Brown can moo! Can you?* New York: Random House.

Eastman, P.D. (2005). *Are you my mother?* New York: Random House.

Ehlert, L. (2000). *Snowballs.* San Diego, CA: Harcourt.

Fujikawa, G. (1980). *Jenny learns a lesson.* New York: Penguin Group.

Galdone, P. (1983). *The gingerbread boy.* Boston: Houghton Mifflin.

Galdone, P. (1984). *The three little pigs*. Boston: Houghton Mifflin.

Galdone, P. (2006). *The little red hen*. Boston: Houghton Mifflin.

Gibbons, G. (1987). *The milk makers*. New York: Aladdin.

Hoberman, M. (2007). *A house is a house for me*. New York: Puffin.

Hutchins, P. (2007). *Barn dance!* New York: Greenwillow.

Jacobson, J. (1997). *Getting to know sharks*. New York: Sadlier-Oxford.

Johnson, C. (1981). *Harold and the purple crayon*. New York: Harper & Row.

Keats, E.J. (1998). *Peter's chair*. New York: Puffin.

Keats, E.J. (1998). *The snowy day*. New York: Puffin.

Lionni, L. (1991). *Frederick*. New York: Random House.

Lionni, L. (2005). *Swimmy*. New York: Knopf.

Mayer, M. (2002). *My trip to the farm*. Columbus, OH: McGraw-Hill.

McCafferty, C. (2001). *The gingerbread man*. Columbus, OH: Brighter Child.

McGovern, A. (1992). *Too much noise*. Boston: Houghton Mifflin.

Pfister, M. (1992). *The rainbow fish*. New York: North-South.

Piper, W. (2005). *The little engine that could*. New York: Platt & Munk.

Potter, B. (2006). *The tale of Peter Rabbit*. New York: Penguin.

Prelutsky, J. (2006). *It's snowing! It's snowing! Winter poems*. New York: HarperCollins.

Prokofiev, S. (2008). *Peter and the wolf*. New York: Penguin Young Readers.

Quackenbush, R.M. (1973). *Go tell Aunt Rhody, starring the old gray goose, who is a living legend in her own lifetime and the greatest American since the American eagle*. Philadelphia: Lippincott.

Satoh, A., & Toda, K. (1996). *Animal faces*. La Jolla, CA: Kane/Miller.

Saunders-Smith, G. (1998). *Autumn*. Mankato, MN: Pebble.

Sendak, M. (1991). *Chicken soup with rice*. New York: Harper & Row.

Sendak, M. (1991). *Pierre*. New York: Harper & Row.

Sendak, M. (1991). *Where the wild things are*. New York: Harper & Row.

Tresselt, M. (1989). *The mitten*. New York: Penguin.

Van Rynbach, I. (2004). *Five little pumpkins*. Honesdale, PA: Boyds Mills.

Willems, M. (2004). *Knuffle bunny*. New York: Hyperion.

Yolen, J. (2007). *Owl moon*. New York: Penguin.

Yolen, J., & Teague, M. (2005). *How do dinosaurs eat their food?* New York: Scholastic.

Zolotow, C. (1977). *Mr. Rabbit and the lovely present*. New York: Harper & Row.

INDEX

Note: Page numbers followed by *f* and *t* indicate figures and tables, respectively.

A

ACTIVITIES: with children's literature, 70*t*–71*t*; for thematic unit, 77–79
AFFLERBACH, P., 43
ALBERTSON, B., 21
ALPHABET BOOKS, 19, 90
ALTERNATIVE LITERACIES, 107–109
AMERICAN LIBRARY ASSOCIATION, 15
ANDERSON, R.C., 5
ANECDOTES OF ACTIVITIES: for evaluation, 34
ANIMALS: books on, 77, 78*t*, 101
ANIMALS AROUND THE WORLD unit, 77–79; books for, 78*t*
APPLEBEE, A.N., 84
ART: activities for thematic units, 78–79; in preschool themes, 74
ASSESSMENT: of children's attitudes towards, 34–35, 37*f*; of children's responses during story readings, 56*f*; child's portfolio for, 35, 65; of concepts of books and comprehension, 64–65, 66*f*–67*f*; definition of, ix; of literacy center time, 34, 36*f*; by parents, 90*f*; of story retelling and rewriting, 60*f*
AUDIO RECORDING–ASSISTED LISTENING: for fluency development, 64
AUDIOTAPES: for evaluation, 34, 65
AUTHOR'S SPOT: in literacy center, 15

B

BARNETT, W.S., 95
BAUMANN, J.F., 44
BIG BOOKS, 1, 8; and concepts of books, 41, 66*f*–67*f*; for library corner, 20; making, 42*f*; on science, 76, 76*f*; in shared reading, 46
BILINGUAL BOOKS, 103
BLANK BOOKS: creating ready-made, 15, 17*f*
BOARD BOOKS, 19
BOOK ILLUSTRATORS, 74
BOOKS: accumulation of, 18; checkout system for, 18, 18*f*; children's attitudes toward, 34–35, 37*f*; concepts of, 39–41; for home, 83–84, 93*t*; for independent reading time, 32; recommended, 97–105; selection of, 20–21; storage of, 15; types of for library corner, 17, 19–21
BRODY, G.H., 5
BUDDY READING, 63; with ELLs, 7
BURNS, M.S., 85
BUS, A.G., 84

C

CALDECOTT MEDAL, 19
CAMPBELL, F.A., 95
CARDBOARD CONCEPT BOOKS, 98
CHAIR OF HONOR: in literacy center, 15
CHALK TALKS, 24, 113
CHANTING, 46. See also choral chanting
CHARACTERS IN CHILDREN'S LITERATURE, 4
CHILDREN'S BOOK COUNCIL, 15
CHILDREN'S LITERATURE: activities for classroom, 70*t*–71*t*; characters in, 4; and child development, 3–5; in curriculum, 69–80; importance of, 1–10; quality of, 21–22; recommended, 97–105; television shows based on, 108–109
CHORAL READING, 8; for fluency development, 64
CLARK, M.M., 6
CLASSROOM VOLUNTEERS, 27, 57
CLOTH BOOKS, 19, 99
COCHRAN-SMITH, M., 86

CHILDREN'S LITERATURE AUTHOR INDEX

Note: Page numbers followed by *t* indicate tables.